FACE
— IN THE —
BOOK

An Overview of the Old Testament
with Wisdom, Direction, and Practical
Applications for Daily Living

Harry C. Washington III

ISBN 978-1-63885-763-1 (Paperback)
ISBN 978-1-63885-764-8 (Digital)

All Scripture quotations, unless otherwise indicated, are taken
from the Holy Bible, New International Version®, NIV®.
Copyright © 1973, 1978, 1984, 2011 by Biblica, Inc.TM
Used by permission of Zondervan. All rights are reserved
worldwide. www.zondervan.com. The "NIV" and "New
International Version" are trademarks registered in the United
States Patent and Trademark Office by Biblica, Inc. TM.

Covenant Books
11661 Hwy 707
Murrells Inlet, SC 29576
www.covenantbooks.com

SPECIAL NOTE

The United States has been ranked as one of the world's worst countries for human trafficking. According to a report by the State Department, the top three nations of origin for victims of human trafficking are the United States, Mexico, and the Philippines.

To help in a small way in the fight against human trafficking in these countries, 100 percent of the profit from this book's sales will go toward the fight against human trafficking. I once read, "If I cannot do great things, I can do small things in a great way" (Martin Luther King Jr).

Thank you for your thirst for learning more about God's Word and for your assistance in fighting human trafficking.

CONTENTS

FOREWORD

Several years ago, I was asked by an older gentleman if I knew the order of all the Old Testament books. Of course, I immediately said, "Yes!" Later, while driving home, I started recalling and reciting the books of the Old Testament. To my surprise, I discovered I didn't know the books of the Old Testament in order—not even close! So I had unknowingly mislead this gentleman.

On this realization, I felt convicted on several levels. Surely I should know them in order. I went to church when I was growing up. I even attended a few Christian colleges. *Wow!* Rather than beat myself up, I saw this lack of knowledge not as a personal failure but as an opportunity to grow.

First things first. Since I knew this gentleman through his granddaughter, I contacted her and asked her to let her grandfather know that I didn't know all the Old Testament books in order. Since I usually see this gentleman once a year at the family Christmas tree farm, I also asked her to let him know that I would be learning all the Old Testament books in order before I saw him next year. I love to challenge myself, so I committed to learning each book of the Old Testament in order while also learning something about each book. I was blessed to visit and to share with him my accomplishment the following year. What a blessing even to this day.

As a result of that one question, I was inspired to write this book and share it with others because I discovered that each book in the Old Testament has practical daily life applications.

PREFACE

I came from a broken home, witnessing things children should never have to witness. These events created trauma within my very core. My childlike innocence was dismantled day after day, week after week, and year after year. There were plenty of sleepless and fearful nights.

In the mornings, when the night terrors were gone, I went to school like most children my age to get an education. Although I was exhausted, the school was a reprieve—until the bell rang to go home. Uncharted waters, violence, broken glass, and drops of blood creating puddles. Where do I turn? Where do I run? Who will help me? Why was I even born? What is my purpose in life? No matter how dark the night and how cloudy the day, I sensed there was always someone right there holding me, comforting me, and protecting me. That someone was God, who showed me my purpose in life.

When I was in my early twenties, I came across this quote, "A hundred years from now it will not matter what my bank account was, the sort of house I lived in, or the kind of car I drove, but the world may be different because I was important in the life of a child" (Forest Witcraft).

Even before I read this quote, as a teenager, I had already realized the positive and negative impact that I had on children my age and younger. I have made it my life's mission to assist young people, especially teenagers, in finding their God-given purpose in life. During my quest to help as many young people as possible, God shifted my course many years ago to include working with adults and the family unit as a whole. I have never forgotten what it was like growing up struggling to find my place in a world that was so confusing. Knowing that God was there in the darkest of nights inspired me to continue to share His goodness by writing this book to help families grow.

Finding the meaning of your existence on planet earth is paramount to living your life with a purpose. God created you, God holds you, God sees you, God knows you, God heals you, God protects you, God comforts you, God directs you, and most importantly, God loves you. God has gifted you with your life. You will get to know Him intimately as you go through the Old Testament.

REFLECTIONS FROM MY CHILDLIKE MIND

As a child, I remember hearing about Jesus, other biblical stories, and their locations. I remember thinking that these stories happened in some far, faraway distant land in another galaxy. If this were the case, then what would all these stories have to do with me?

When I was a child, I lived in England for three years. I lived in what I thought was a mansion. We had tall fences in the backyard with a flagpole that almost touched the sky from my view. On the other side of the fence was a vast alley bordered by another fence separating it from the neighbor's yard.

Many years later, as an adult, I was blessed to go back to my mansion in England. When I got there, I walked down the alley leading to my backyard. To my amazement, I could extend my arms and almost touch both my old fence and the neighbor's fence across the alley. With ease, I was able to look over this "tall fence," and my flagpole to the sky seemed to have shrunk considerably. I could now stand and touch the top of the flagpole. At this moment, I was somewhat disappointed and shocked. Then I started laughing at myself for being so naïve and foolish. As for the mansion, you guessed it—wasn't a mansion at all.

The point I'm making is that the property hadn't changed. The difference was I had grown up. As you mature, you realize that some of your past perceptions are not always something you can rely on. Have you ever heard of the Easter bunny or the tooth fairy? As you get older, you have to reevaluate things you have been taught.

Is December 25th Christ's birthday? Is Santa Claus real? Is Jesus real? Is Bethlehem of Judea a real place? Was Mary, the mother of Jesus, pregnant and still a virgin? How? You see, in our lives, things can be a bit confusing. What is real? Well, Bethlehem is a real place; Jesus is real and was born of a virgin by the mighty work of God. The birthplace is not in a far, faraway galaxy. As a matter of fact, Bethlehem of Judea is the birthplace of Jesus. This little town still exists today and is situated 6.2 miles south of Jerusalem in the Middle East.

From Knoxville, Tennessee, to Jerusalem by plane would take anywhere from fifteen to twenty hours. What a fantastic thing to think about. I could be in the same town where Jesus was born over two thousand years ago in less than twenty-four hours. Is that amazing or what? God is *good!* Many people, both young and old, still have a child-like mind when it comes to knowing and understanding the Old Testament. Do you have a childlike mind when it comes to dealing with the Old Testament?

God's plan for us is contained in the first book in the Bible, Genesis, through the last book of the Bible, Revelation. Throughout each subsequent book, God has given us a lamp and a road map with directions that lead to Him forever as our final destination. God's word is a lamp to our feet and a light for our path (Psalm 119:105). Hold on to the lamp as together we travel down God's path for our lives.

ACKNOWLEDGMENTS

Writing a book is more challenging than I thought and more rewarding than I could have ever imagined. None of this would have been possible without my best friend, my Lord and my Savior, Jesus Christ. There were hundreds of times throughout this process I thought about quitting. However, there was one thought that always kept me going. This thought was that Jesus never gave up on me.

I'm eternally grateful to my soulmate, best friend, and a true gift from God, my adorable wife, Audrey. Throughout all the storms of life, our love for each other is the strongest it's ever been and continues to get stronger with each passing day. Thank you, best friend.

One day about seventeen years ago, God gave Audrey and me a lifelong blessing. Her name is Laura Patera. She is undeniably our most trusted, loyal, faithful friend, and most importantly, our beautiful sister in Jesus. Thank you, Laura, for who you are and whose you are. I praise God for Laura Patera and her family.

I'm also forever grateful to God for the angel He chose to give birth to me. My lovely mother, Cynthia Dorthia Gomez, also known as my Mamado and Sister Go-Go by some of her church family. Although Mamado is no longer on the earth in the flesh, she is forever in the arms of

Jesus and in my heart. Thank You, God, and thank you, Mamado, for your unconditional love for me. I will see you both in the resurrection.

I would also like to thank all my brothers and sisters from the following churches of Christ: North Broadway (my loving and nurturing childhood congregation), Waynesville, Outreach, Kentucky Avenue, Woodland, Davis, and Karns. Thank you for sharing your lives with Audrey and me.

I am thankful for all my family members and friends who have been a part of my life here on earth. Both positive and negative interactions have helped shape and mold me into the Christian man I am today. Thank You! God is *real*! Seek Him only!

I would like to thank all of those who will purchase and read *Face in the Book*. I would like to also thank those who will share this book with others. I know that God already knows whose life will be enriched by this book.

Thank You, God, for placing on my heart that 100 percent of the profit from the sales of this book should be used to support the fight against human trafficking.

Last but definitely not least, to every person who has been instrumental in assisting me with the process of writing this book. The names are too numerous to list. However, you know who you are, and most importantly, God knows who you are. A special thank-you to all of you!

INTRODUCTION

Have you ever talked with someone who gave you a detailed explanation about why they didn't like a particular movie, yet when you watched this same movie, you thoroughly enjoyed it? And later, you discover that despite all their reasons, it turns out that they never even watched the movie. Instead, their disapproval was based entirely on the negative persuasion of others. Have you ever heard people speak negatively about books, only to find out they never read them, and they based criticism on hearsay? Think of what you would have missed if you had allowed others' opinions to influence you.

While you are still pondering, let's consider how you can take in false information and unqualified opinions. While everyone lacks knowledge to a certain degree, are you among those who choose to stay uneducated and uninformed?

One of the Old Testament prophets you will learn about is Hosea. He informed the people of his day that they are "destroyed for lack of knowledge" (Hosea 4:6) Our responsibility is to gain knowledge and wisdom for ourselves and not rely totally on others' information.

The vast majority of people I have met on five different continents have become victims of unqualified opinions.

They spent years relying on others' opinions, being people pleasers, which ultimately left them spiritually bankrupt, broken, empty, confused, frustrated, angry, resentful, and even suicidal. Their lives were wasted because they chased material items that ultimately corrupted their spirits.

I've also lived many years searching for joy in useless material and physical pleasures. It was like trying to catch the wind. After many years of being involved in nursing homes, hospitals, schools, the military, and even churches, I often witnessed this misfortune. As a counselor for over forty years, I clocked many hours peering behind the scenes of people's lives. I listened to precious souls who were empty, fearful, and bewildered, wondering what had happened to their lives. Many have shared that they wished they could go back and live life over again. Unfortunately, our lives are not like a video game equipped with a reset button. Once our life is over, it is over.

This is why I am sharing godly wisdom with those who are seeking God. I want to help others avoid the major pitfalls that Satan uses to deceive, destroy, and dismantle lives. God has a master plan and an excellent road map for your life, as you will read in the Old Testament.

Please understand! I do not want to sound like everyone I ever encountered continues living an unchanged life. *Absolutely not!* Words like *restoration* and *reconciliation* are not just words to God. They are significant realities for you and me.

So why write a book about the Old Testament? I once heard something like this: write a book that you wish you had read. This book is the book I wish I had as a teenager or as a young adult to help me understand the importance of the Old Testament.

I am excited to share some of the practical knowledge, wisdom, and understanding gifted to me. I've found hundreds of practical applications from the Old Testament that I apply to my daily life. You may be wondering why I place so much emphasis on the thirty-nine books of the Old Testament.

The Bible has sixty-six books divided into two sections: the Old Testament and the New Testament. There are thirty-nine books in the Old Testament and twenty-seven books in the New Testament.

It is impossible to have a precise percentage of how much of the Bible consists of the Old Testament; however, most estimate between 70 and 80 percent. When you miss 70 to 80 percent of anything, especially God's story, don't you think that you are missing out on a lot of valuable life-changing information that God wants you to know?

The Old Testament can be very confusing and intimidating, and I want to help you understand it through this overview. Just like your body has a skeletal system, the Old Testament is similar. It also has what I like to call "the skeletal layout." I ask that you use this book as a study guide. It is designed to be an aid and not a substitute for the Bible, so it is most helpful to have your Bible open when studying.

As you study, you will find that the scriptures are filled with examples that will help you understand how to live a fulfilled life. Imagine that you are sitting next to the author of a book you are reading. It is just the two of you alone for hours, and you have permission to ask him questions about what he meant when he wrote his book. Since God left His word down here for you, He will indeed sit next to you to help you understand His book. It is as simple as asking Him through prayer.

As you will see in each book, there are sample prayers, practical applications, and verses selected for golden nuggets (valuable thoughts). I want to encourage you to pray for what is in your heart, choose practical applications that will foster growth for you, and obtain golden nuggets that will enrich your soul.

UNDERSTANDING THE LAYOUT OF THE OLD TESTAMENT

Before we start our study and survey of the Old Testament, it's crucial to understand the layout of the thirty-nine Old Testament books in our Bible.

I like to say that the Old Testament has five categories and eight major events. In this guide, we are going to look at the individual books in each category.

The five categories:

1. Books of Moses—five books (also called the Pentateuch)
2. History of Israel—twelve books
3. Poetry and Wisdom—five books
4. Major Prophets—five books
5. Minor Prophets—twelve books

From the above five categories, you see that the books in the Old Testament are grouped in a sequence of 5-12-5-5-12. I like to refer to this sequence as "the combination" to help unlock the structure of the Old Testament. When you turn to the table of contents in your Bible, the first five books are known as "the Book of Moses." These books are generally in chronological order. Beginning with the sixth book, we enter a sequence of twelve historical books that continues where Deuteronomy left off. The history of Israel is the primary focus of this section.

The next set of five books in the Old Testament are the books of poetry and wisdom, followed by another collection of five books called the major prophets. Major prophets does not mean they are more important than the minor prophets. The name refers to the size of their books, which are significantly larger than those of the minor prophets.

The final sequence of twelve Old Testament books is the minor prophets. It must also be noted that some events overlap within this five-fold division and are repeated in books in one of the other divisions. The order is simple yet very significant.

Now that we've discussed the five Old Testament categories, let's look at what I refer to as eight significant events that will occur during our journey through the Old Testament.

1. *Creation*—You will learn about Adam, Eve, Noah, and the flood.
2. *Abraham*—You will learn about the beginning of the nation of Israel, beginning with Abraham, Isaac, and Jacob.
3. *Moses*—You learn about how God provided Israel a way out of slavery, along with forty years of wilderness wanderings before entering the promised land.

4. *Joshua*—You learn how God used a mighty military leader to fulfill God's promise by giving Israel the land promised to Abraham.
5. *Judges*—You learn about some amazing heroes and how fickle people can be regarding their service and worship of God.
6. *Kings*—You learn that God gave Israel the kings they asked for and what the results were.
7. *Taken into Captivity*—You will learn why God's people were taken captive from the "promised land" and God's part in it.
8. *Return from Captivity*—You learn about the events that led to God's people being allowed to return to their homeland.

I encourage you to memorize this structure because it will help your understanding as you grow in God's teachings.

Quick Review

The combination of the Old Testament books is 5-12-5-5-12.

Here is what I teach to help people remember some of the significant events of the Old Testament. C-A-M, then J-J-Kings. C-Creation, A-Abraham, M-Moses, J-Joshua, J-Judges, and Kings and the last two events: "Taken into Captivity" and "Released from Captivity."

Please do not be overly concerned if you cannot remember these events in order. I have designed this book as a guide to assist you with clarification as you travel through each particular book.

Here is an important sidenote. You will see that I used some scriptures from the New Testament. I've ~~did~~ done this to show that the Old Testament paves the way for Jesus in the New Testament. Equally important is to understand that the New Testament is the fulfillment of prophecies found in the Old Testament.

Now, without further ado, let us hoist our sails and prepare to navigate the sea of books in the Old Testament.

BOOKS OF
MOSES

GENESIS

Outline of the Book of Genesis

1. Creation—Genesis 1:1–2:3
2. Adam and Eve—Genesis 2:4–5:32
3. The first prophecy about Jesus—Genesis 3:15
4. Noah and the ark—Genesis 6:1–11:32
5. Promise told to Abraham that he would be the father of a great nation and is told to sacrifice his son, Isaac—Genesis 12:1–25:18
6. Isaac's story—Genesis 25:19–28:9
7. Jacob's story and how he wrestles with God—Genesis 28:10–36:43
8. Joseph was mistreated by his brothers, sold, falsely accused of sexual assault, and placed in prison—Genesis 37:1–40:23
9. Pharaoh's dream, Joseph freed, his dreams came true, and eventually, he was laid to rest—Genesis 41:1–50:26

Genesis, as the name implies, is the book of beginnings. As human beings, we have a sentimental attachment to beginnings. Have you ever seen a newborn baby? Everyone is usually happy because they love the new beginning a baby represents. We also have a natural curiosity regarding our origins and how it all began.

In Genesis, we have insight into how God created all things. This is why God instructed Moses to write these five books. Knowing our hunger for knowledge of our beginnings, God laid a firm foundation for us to build our lives from the very beginning of creation.

Genesis deals with questions that humanity has been asking for years. It reveals the beginning of everything. It talks about how God created the universe and all living things, including humankind. Genesis reveals God's original plan for populating the earth and the unique relationship He wants to have with His children.

It shows how even when God's creation rebelled against Him, God was gracious enough and made a way for His children to come back to Him. Genesis then reveals how God goes about keeping His promises by focusing on a single family's bloodline to bring forth Jesus as our Savior. Following this single family's bloodline is remarkable. It leads directly to Jesus. By following the teaching of Jesus, you will become divinely connected to His unbroken family bloodline. *Exciting—amazing and unbelievable.*

We learn about Adam and Eve, our first parents, and the events that led to their separation from God. Before their separation, they lived in a paradise where everything they needed was provided. They only had one restriction: not to eat of the tree of knowledge of good and evil. Sadly, the serpent or devil tempted Eve, and she ate the *forbidden fruit.* Then she gave it to Adam, who also ate. As a result of this disobedience, God had to cast them out of paradise. Their sin is often referred to as "the original sin." This sin has affected every generation from that day on. All sin, just like Adam's and Eve's, stems from one source, disobedience.

Approximately nine generations after Adam's death, God decided to destroy all of humanity with a flood because the people had grown increasingly evil. Out of the entire human population, only eight people were saved because of their faithfulness to God. They were Noah and his family. After the flood, God used Noah's three sons and their wives to repopulate this world in which we live. The study of Noah's sons repopulating our world is a fascinating study to do. I guarantee you that your life will truly be enriched. You will get a better understanding of the cultures and their different geographical locations. As you will read, Genesis is monumental in answering questions about our humanity.

Up to this point, God was focused on humanity as a whole. Then, in Genesis 12:17, God makes a covenant (agreement) with our forefather, Abraham. God begins to focus on this single family. Abraham will have many descendants who will form a great nation, a people through whom salvation would come. This promise would be fulfilled in Abraham's greatest descendant, Jesus. The purpose of this covenant is a binding promise of far-reaching importance, for it reveals God's only hope for us today!

The promise given to Abraham was passed down through the generations. After Abraham, it was passed down to his son Isaac, who passed it down to his son Jacob. Jacob had twelve sons whose descendants became known as the twelve tribes of Israel. In Genesis 32:28, God changed Jacob's name to Israel. Keep in mind this name change. It will *significantly help* you understand so many verses when you read the Bible. Remember this: all these tribes are related, starting as Jacob/Israel's twelve sons. Throughout the generations to come, regardless of whether they were from north or south, they were all related, all Israelites, all Jewish, all Hebrews. So when you read any of these names, Jews, Jewish, Israelites, and Hebrews, they are all the same group of people just referred to by different names.

Genesis also shows us examples of sin, such as hatred, murder, drunkenness, lust, unhealthy family relationships, greed, cheating, irresponsibility, dishonesty, jealousy, and violence, to name a few.

Are the above all that we can learn from this first book of the Old Testament? Definitely not! Genesis is extensive in the wealth of material it contains for exposing human nature and how we can regain that amazing paradise that was lost.

I cannot possibly outline in detail all the lessons in each book of the Old Testament. However, here are some crucial facts to remember as you continue your journey through the rest of the Old Testament books. In Genesis, God gives us a clear plan. He promised He would restore humankind through the Israelite nation, especially through the tribe of Judah (one of the twelve sons named Judah). Guess what tribe Jesus came from? The Bible speaks for itself. I am so thankful that Jesus came to help all of us to live a life free of the power and penalty of sin. Amen!

My Verses for Golden Nuggets

> Then God said, "Let us make man-
> kind in our image, in our likeness."
> (Genesis 1:26)

> In the beginning was the Word, and
> the Word was with God, and the Word
> was God. (John 1:1)

These verses are powerful because they show Jesus
was with God in the beginning, and together they created
all things.

> I will surely bless you and make your
> descendants as numerous as the stars in
> the sky and as the sand on the seashore.
> Your descendants will take possession of
> the cities of their enemies, and through
> your offspring, all nations on earth will
> be blessed, because you have obeyed me.
> (Genesis 22:17–18)

God promised Abraham that his descendants would
be as numerous as the stars in the sky and the sand on the
seashore. He kept his promise, and we are living proof of
that because we are descendants (stars) of Abraham. How?

> So in Christ Jesus, you are all children
> of God through faith, for all of you who

were baptized into Christ have clothed yourselves with Christ. There is neither Jew nor Gentile, neither slave nor free, nor is there male and female, for you are all one in Christ Jesus. If you belong to Christ, then you are Abraham's seed, and heirs according to the promise. (Galatians 3:26–29)

Once again, I'm using scriptures from the New Testament (John and Galatians) to show how the Old Testament and New Testament go hand in hand, complementing each other to fulfill promises as God intended.

Practical Applications for Your Life Today

- God is still fulfilling His promises today and allows you to become descendants/stars of Abraham.
- God's master plan for you includes love, hope, forgiveness, and healing.
- No matter how far you have fallen into the pit of moral filth, God's hand is extended to lift you out—take it!
- God is faithful in keeping His promises. Forgiveness is yours for the taking.
- You are like Adam and Eve because your beginning came from God.
- Just as Adam and Eve lived and died, you will have the very same fate. "And as it is appointed

unto men once to die, but after this the judgment" (Hebrews 9:27 KJV).

- Genesis is all about the daily choices people made and how those choices impacted them and subsequent generations. The same is true for your daily choices. Your choices will direct the course of your life and determine your eternal destination.

Prayer

Heavenly Father, help me make choices today to show You I am interested in seeking You with all my heart. Help me know that Your promises are authentic and freely given to me as I choose to honor You in my daily choices. I don't need to be perfect. I just need Jesus as my perfect Savior. In Jesus' name, I pray. Amen.

*****

I hope you learned a lot in this first book of the Old Testament. I hope you saw how God laid the foundation of this world and how everything else panned out from Genesis; that alone is a big lesson. God's plan is to love you, comfort you, guide you, and to protect you.

EXODUS

Outline of the Book of Exodus

1. Israel enslaved in Egypt—Exodus 1:1–22
2. God chooses Moses—Exodus 2:1–4:31
3. God chooses Moses to free Israel—Exodus 5:1–7:13
4. The ten plagues—Exodus 7:14–11:10
5. The Passover—Exodus 12:1–30
6. The Exodus from Egypt—Exodus 12:31–13:16
7. Crossing the Red Sea—Exodus 13:17–15:21
8. Complaining in the desert—Exodus 15:22–18:27
9. The Ten Commandments and the giving of the law—Exodus 19:1–24:18
10. The tabernacle instructions—Exodus 25:1–31:18
11. Breaking the law—Exodus 32:1–34:35
12. Tabernacle construction—Exodus 35:1–40:38

Throughout life, we will have times when we find ourselves at a crossroads where we have to move, escape, exit, or make a departure. Regardless of the word you choose to describe these events, they all say the same thing—you are making an exodus.

You may have moved from an apartment or a home. Perhaps you escaped from being in a bad relationship or departed from an institution such as a jail, a hospital, or even a school. I remember my exodus from the United States Air Force when I retired after twenty years of service. Retiring gave me a new start with health benefits and a guaranteed paycheck for the rest of my life. Praise God!

The same way we enjoy new beginnings, we can enjoy happy departures and exoduses as well. However, with every exodus, there is nearly always a reason behind it. This was the case with the children of Israel.

Genesis ended with the twelve sons of Jacob/Israel moving to Egypt to escape a worldwide famine (extreme scarcity of food). Joseph's leadership ability helped Egypt prepare for a natural disaster. Because of this, the Pharaoh (Egyptian ruler) welcomed Joseph's family with open arms and gave them the very best of Egypt's land. This is how Genesis ends.

A *very significant fact* to keep in mind is that around four hundred years occurred between Genesis 50, the last chapter, and the first chapter in Exodus. Many people reading the two books make the mistake of assuming Exodus is an immediate continuation of Genesis without considering this four-hundred-year gap.

By the time Exodus was written, none of the original twelve sons were alive. "Now Joseph and all his brothers and all that generation died" (Exodus 1:6). This is very important because, from the book of Exodus on, members of the twelve tribes are all descendants of Jacob's original twelve sons. Failure to keep this in mind will cause you mass confusion.

Following Joseph's death, a new Pharaoh came to the throne who "knew not Joseph." He greatly enslaved and abused God's people, forcing them to work on backbreaking, gut-wrenching building projects. With God's perfect timing, he selected an unlikely candidate to lead his people out of slavery in Egypt (Africa). Moses was called by God to lead the Israelites from Egypt to the land of Canaan located in today's Middle East. Remember, this is the land that God promised to Abraham.

God called Moses by appearing to him in a burning bush. Here God showed Moses His power by making Moses' hand leprous and then healing his hand. He also turned Moses' rod into a venomous snake.

In his new God-given leadership role, Moses appeared to Pharaoh and the people of Egypt, declaring a message from God, "Let my people go!" When they refused to listen to God's command, the Lord allowed ten plagues to come upon the Egyptians.

The last plague involved the killing of all the firstborn males in Egypt, regardless of their age. The only way for the Israelites to be spared from this plague was to kill a lamb and spread its blood on the doorposts of their houses. After this horrific night of death, the Egyptians thrust the Israelites out, and the Israelites left in haste. This is why the Passover is so significant.

Passover is one of the most important religious festivals. Jews celebrate the Feast of Passover to remember the liberation of the children of Israel. When death came that night, it passed over the homes with the blood from the lamb on their doorposts.

After the Israelites were gone, Pharaoh had a change of heart and went after them. The Israelites were facing the enormous Red Sea in front of them and an angry Egyptian army behind them. Imagine the anger that each man had, whose firstborn son had died, including the Pharaoh's son. Pharaoh was set up for a classic military maneuver when God helped the Israelites escape the Egyptian army by parting the Red Sea, enabling the Israelites to walk across the seabed on dry ground. When Pharaoh and his army pursued them going into the Red Sea, we see God's perfect timing once again. After the *last* Israelite was safe on the other side, God ended the miracle, drowning Pharaoh and his whole army.

From then on, God moved along with the Israelites, guiding them by using a cloud pillar during the day and a pillar of fire at night. Even this showed God's care for His children. God wanted to be with His children 24-7, 365.

God led them to Mount Sinai, where He first appeared to Moses. There God showed His love by giving Moses the Ten Commandments, ordaining Moses' brother Aaron as a priest, and giving the people instructions to build a tabernacle (a movable habitation, a place of worship for God's people). By doing all this, God officially established Israel, not just as a people but as a nation. This tabernacle was a place to worship, and it provided a place for God to dwell with them. The Ten Commandments were instructions for this new nation. They now needed to know how God expected them to live their lives and how to structure their leadership.

My Verses for Golden Nuggets

> God said to Moses, "I AM Who I AM. This is what you are to say to the Israelites: 'I AM has sent me to you.'" God also said to Moses, "Say to the Israelites, 'The Lord, the God of your fathers—the God of Abraham, the God of Isaac and the God of Jacob—has sent me to you.' This is my name forever, the name by which I AM to be remembered from generation to generation." (Exodus 3:14–15)

These verses make me smile because it's so simple yet so mighty. Who sent you? "*I AM*" has sent me. God, to me, is the Great I AM! Who is I AM to you?

Practical Applications for Your Life Today

- God offers you an exit plan, a way of escape from whatever dangers, trials, or heartaches you may face. Your part is to choose the exit plan God has provided for you.
- He provides a way of departure from the slave master of sin—Satan, the Pharaoh of all pharaohs.
- God will go through extreme measures to save you.
- Look up right now; is it day or night? Regardless of whether it's day or night, your God is willing to guide you.

- God's timing for you is perfect, so don't wait any longer to follow Him closely.
- God hears all your prayers and is willing to guide you.
- Preparation for leadership takes patience, time, and willingness to follow God's instructions.
- Despite your imperfections, God wants to use you, just like He used Aaron and Moses.
- God always allows you to make U-turns (repentance). Change your attitude, and your behaviors will follow.
- You have no acceptable excuses for lack of action and unfaithfulness in your daily life.
- You are provided with a landslide of daily choices. God supplies you with everything you need. "But my God shall supply all your need according to his riches in glory by Christ Jesus" (Philippians 4:19 KJV).

Prayer

Heavenly Father, thank You for the many true stories of loving, leading, and caring for Your people. Thank You for Your perfect timing. God, only You, the great I AM, can provide me with the help, strength, wisdom, and guidance that I need. In Jesus' name, I pray. Amen.

*****

As we come to the end of the book of Exodus, I hope that you will apply godly principles in your life. It takes courage to be willing to identify those things in your life that are keeping you captive. Seek God's guidance as you identify the things holding you captive, and trust in God to provide you with an exit plan and godly leadership. Take the exit plan by following His guidelines, striving to have God help you in every area of your life. God always provides people with guidelines, plans, and even laws. Speaking of laws, this is what the next book is all about—God's laws.

LEVITICUS

Outline of the Book of Leviticus

1. Instructions for offerings—Leviticus 1–7
2. Instructions for God's priests—Leviticus 8–10
3. Instructions for God's people—Leviticus 11–15
4. Instructions for the altar and the Day of Atonement—Leviticus 16
5. Practical holiness—Leviticus 17–22
6. Sabbaths, seasons, festivals, and feasts—Leviticus 23–25
7. Conditions for receiving God's blessing—Leviticus 26–27

How vital are laws? Have you ever imagined all the horrific things that would happen if we had no legal system?

Even you and I know the importance of the role laws play in our society. Without them, we would be living in a state of disorder and chaos. Can you picture driving on our roads and highways without any traffic laws? Traffic signals would be worthless because you could make the colors mean whatever you wanted. Would any of us dare venture out?

In reality, there is no such thing as no laws. Even street gangs have their own "laws" or codes to live by. We are all under some form of law in some way; the question is, whose laws?

When God blessed the Israelites with the exodus from Egypt, they had a new beginning as a nation, and they had the Ten Commandments as their foundational law. God found Moses and the nation of Israel worthy of being handed His laws. God understands the vital role laws play in society. People need structure!

The children of Israel had just made it across the Red Sea out of slavery. There needed to be spiritual leaders and guidelines for their new nation to function.

The book of Leviticus is named after the Levites, descendants of Levi, one of the twelve sons of Jacob/Israel. The Levites were the tribe God chose to be priests and care for the tabernacle. While some parts of Leviticus give instructions for the priests and Levites, the book is addressed to Israel's entire nation. Leviticus is written to detail God's presence with the people and how He expects them to live.

Remember the tabernacle was a portable tent for worship, a place where God dwelled during their wilderness wanderings. God had precise instructions regarding the tabernacle, including which Levites were allowed to do specific duties. The tabernacle had to be kept holy or set apart for God because He would not dwell among anything unclean or defiled. The people living around the tabernacle also had to be holy so they would not contaminate God's dwelling place with their sin. Leviticus gave instructions to follow and explained what people should do when they sinned. Sin required a sacrifice of some kind.

The priests dealt with the animal blood sacrifices the people offered to make restitution for their sinful, broken state. The laws given in Leviticus were meant to direct and acquaint the people with God's forgiving and compassionate character. Leviticus shows us that God wants to have a personal relationship with His people. As part of this relationship, God always provides His people with guidelines and directions. When it comes to knowing what God expects, He has always been very clear. He still, without exception, guides those who are genuinely searching for Him.

There have been times when I experienced being brokenhearted, lonely, depressed, burdened down with worry, suffering losses, feeling helpless, hopeless, and being sin-sick. No matter what state or condition I was in, God's healing hand was always extended, waiting for me to take hold.

"I AM" will be with you always, even until the end of the world (Matthew 28:20 KJV). We all are going to be faced with hard times. I am thankful that "I AM" has said He will always be with me. However, the real question is, are we willing to trust God and be with Him? I am, how about you? The Israelites had to be willing to be with God according to His laws.

God's character has always been to love humanity by providing avenues to stay in a correct relationship with Him. Have you ever wondered why we do not offer up animal sacrifices today? Here is why. It is because God loved you and me so much that He offered up His only son Jesus, as the ultimate and perfect sacrifice for our sins. "Behold! The Lamb of God who takes away the sin of the world!" (John 1:29 NKJV) Thank You, Jesus!

The Israelites were helpless slaves in Egypt, just like we are hopelessly in slavery within our own lives without God's sacrificial *lamb*, Jesus. No Jesus! No Lamb! No Sacrifice! No Forgiveness! Equals a *POW* (prisoner of within). Let God be our deliverer.

My Verses for Golden Nuggets

> Be holy because I, the Lord your God, am holy. (Leviticus 19:2)

> But just as he who called you is holy, so be holy in all you do; for it is written: "Be holy, because I am holy." (1 Peter 1:15–16)

> This poor man cried out, and the LORD heard him and saved him out of all his troubles. (Psalm 34:6)

There is no way that God expects you to be holy and perfect in your flesh, for God knows that you would fail. However, you become holy when you have surrendered your life over to Jesus, the perfect sacrifice for your sins.

Practical Applications for Your Life Today

- It should be great news to you to know you are never alone because all have sinned and violated God's guidelines.
- Jesus is the Lamb of God, the perfect sacrifice. His blood will cleanse you from all your sins. Live with and for Him.
- Jesus wants to be your *ultimate high priest*—what a privilege!
- Today God is very serious about how to worship Him. "God is a Spirit: and they that worship Him must worship Him in Spirit and truth" (John 4:24 KJV).
- God has provided you with His words in the Bible, giving you His guidelines, laws, and expectations.
- God graciously provided you with examples of how your faithful obedience gets His full attention.
- God's love for you is seen in the way He guides, leads, and instructs.
- Do not feel you can treat God as a mathematical equation: $1+1 = 2$. Living for God is not about a formula; it's about a relationship.
- God answers your prayers in three ways: "Yes!" "No!" or "Not right now!"

Prayer

Dear God, I need Your guidance in my life. I believe You have been guiding and directing people from the beginning. My life will never be complete without You. I know that I have let things get in the way of drawing closer to You. Please help me improve my relationship with You by being more conscious of Your purpose and protection for my life. In Jesus' name, I pray. Amen.

*****

I believe your journey thus far is starting to take shape. First, you learned about how God created everything in the book of Genesis. Next, you learned how God's people were taken into slavery and how God led them out of slavery through Moses. In this book, you learned how God gave His people laws to guide them so they don't have to fall into slavery again.

The major takeaway from Leviticus is that God loves and cares deeply for every human being. This is shown again in our next book, where God asks everyone to give an account for themselves.

NUMBERS

Outline of the Book of Numbers

1. The people wandered in the desert for forty years until the faithless generation was consumed—Numbers 15:1–21, 35

2. Balaam, a local sorcerer and prophet, attempted to curse God's people as they entered the promised land, but God only allowed Balaam to bless them—Numbers 22:1–25:18

3. Moses takes another census of the people to organize an army—Numbers 26:1–27:11

4. Moses appoints Joshua as his successor—Numbers 27:12–22

5. God gives instructions on offerings and feasts—Numbers 28:1–30:16

6. The Israelites take vengeance on the Midianites, then camped on the plains of Moab—Numbers 31:1–36:13

In Exodus and Leviticus, you learned how God handed down His laws and guidelines to direct and protect His people. If you think the whole thing ended there, you need to think again. God not only handed His laws to Moses;

He also made sure His people followed those laws. God is an accountant, and He loves keeping account of His people. As the name of the book suggests, God called for a roll call, a headcount. It was once said that "God loves you so much that He can't take His eyes off of you." Let's learn more about the all-seeing God in the book of Numbers!

Like our census today, the first section of the book of Numbers details an accounting of the number of Israelites. Following the census, God gave Moses his marching orders to prepare for battle using men twenty years old and older. God put a spy mission in place before the people went into battle. Moses selected twelve spies to go into the Promised Land (located in today's Middle East) to size up the strength of the enemy.

Upon returning, ten of the spies were fearful and gave a very negative report. They said God's people were "like grasshoppers" compared to the Promised Land's tall giants. Only two spies, Joshua and Caleb, insisted they could take the land. Sadly, the people refused to listen to Joshua and Caleb, allowing contagious fear to spread throughout the army like wildfire, destroying their morale. Fear shifted the people's focus from the greatness of God to the size of their enemy.

Since this fear paralyzed all the men twenty years of age and older, all of them except Joshua and Caleb were given a slow death sentence. Because the Israelites disobeyed God by listening to their fear, they could not enter the Promised Land. They wandered around in the wilderness for forty years around Mount Sinai while God waited for each man in this generation to die before allowing the

Israelites to advance to the Promised Land. This is why the Hebrew meaning of this book is "in the wilderness."

While in the wilderness, God showed the people His patience, kindness, and discipline. Joshua and Caleb were the only two spies who did not die in the wilderness because they focused their belief on God's strength and power. God honored their courage and faithfulness and allowed the two of them to live and eventually enter the Promised Land.

As God helped the Israelites escape the bondage of slavery, He also provided them with responsibilities. The same is true for you. When you escape the bondage of being a slave to sin, God gives you the responsibility to take action and continue moving forward. Have you ever seen a dog chasing its tail? It's pretty funny but also quite senseless. This is what happened to the Israelites.

Since, they became fearful, they wandered around the wilderness for forty years. Have you had times where you became paralyzed with fear or maybe you are currently living in fear? Keep reading, and ask God to increase your faith. Increased faith will always cancel out your fears.

Do you have an accountability partner, someone you can confide in to help you grow stronger in your faith? I hope so! But if not, as one of my childhood heroes on television, Mr. T, would say, "I pity the fool." For far too many years, I was this pitiful fool, wandering around in the wilderness of my mind trying to hide and conceal my sins, never realizing that concealing was detrimental to my psychological, emotional, physical, and spiritual health. I was deteriorating, not leaving any room for healing. It wasn't until I chose to have accountability partners, went to meetings, and sought out counseling for some of my sinful struggles that my freedom and healing began.

"Therefore, confess your sins to each other and pray for each other so that you may be healed. The prayer of a righteous person is powerful and effective" (James 5:16).

Having godly accountability and transparency is absolutely essential for real spiritual growth and healing. It was once said, "You are only as sick as your secrets, and if you conceal them, you can never be healed." Often people allow their pride to get in the way of seeking help. God gives us insight into how He feels about pride. God is against a prideful person; however, He shows favor to the humble (James 4:6).

Do you want God's favor? Be humble and ask for help in dealing with your wilderness. Fortunately, we can learn some valuable lessons while wandering in our wilderness. The number one thing I learned is that even with my failures, I can count on God, and He is counting on me to be open and transparent. This is the type of relationship God wants to have with you. Remember that God has your number, and He is always calling you. The question is, are you going to answer His call or let it go to voicemail?

What are your present circumstances? Are you currently wandering in your wilderness, or are you being more than a conqueror in your life with Christ? I know how you got into your current circumstances. That's easy—by your choices. Now is the time to pick up the phone (His Word) and listen to His instructions. Remember, He is not far from you, and He's waiting to hear from you.

My Verse for Golden Nuggets

> But the Lord said to Moses and Aaron, "Because you did not trust in me enough to honor me as holy in the sight of the Israelites, you will not bring this community into the land I give them." (Numbers 20:12)

This verse speaks fairness to me. Today your primary purpose should not be to try to understand everything about God but to trust God in everything.

Practical Applications for Your Life Today

- God has your number, and there is no need to hide and make excuses.
- Stand up and be counted faithful and live forever.
- Don't focus on the size of your enemy. Instead, focus on the power and promises of God.
- In every situation, ask yourself, are you living in fear or living by faith? Live your dreams, not your fears.
- Are you wandering in your wilderness or marching in God's kingdom of love?
- Who and what has the most influence on your life? Social media? Netflix? Television? Are you following the ways of the world like the majority? Or have you committed to living for God?

- God plus one (you) equals the majority, and a million men without God is the minority.

Gradually, we are coming to the end of the *Books of Moses*. I sincerely hope you are allowing God's teachings to sail into your soul and provide you with hope for a better future.

> "For I know the plans I have for you," declares the LORD, "plans to prosper you and not to harm you, plans to give you hope and a future. Then you will call on me and come and pray to me, and I will listen to you. You will seek me and find me when you seek me with all your heart." (Jeremiah 29:1–13)

Do you want a better future? If yes, then you have done well for yourself. Keep sailing.

In this book, you learned that fear and walking in the wilderness go hand in hand and that this is not part of God's plan for His children. Twelve spies went out, and when they came back, who did the men of Israel listen to? The ten (which is the majority) or the two (the minority)? In your life today, are you following the majority in the world's ways or the few in God's ways?

> Do not love the world or anything in the world. If anyone loves the world, love for the Father is not in them. For

everything in the world the lust of the flesh, the lust of the eyes, and the pride of life—comes not from the Father but from the world. The world and its desires pass away, but whoever does the will of God lives forever. (1 John 2:15–17)

It is a tough challenge not to fall prey to the desires of this world. God is willing to help you become more than a conqueror in your life. In the next book, God repeats His laws to His children after they spent many years in the wilderness because of their disobedience. Let's see if they listened to God this time. The next destination we are sailing to is the book of Deuteronomy.

Prayer

Dearest Heavenly Father, thank You for the examples of wandering around in the wilderness. I just read how people who were disobedient to You wasted their lives by living in a cycle of doing the same thing over and over. They could not move forward in their lives until they were willing to follow You and You alone. Help me, Father, to address my wilderness thoughts and behaviors that hinder me from moving forward into my blessings of being Your respectable child. In Jesus' name, I pray. Amen.

DEUTERONOMY

Outline of the Book of Deuteronomy

1. Moses' first speech about Israel's history— Deuteronomy 1:6–4:43
2. Moses talks about the basic requirements of the Law—Deuteronomy 4:44–11:32
3. Moses' second speech detailed the requirements of the Law—Deuteronomy 12:1–26:19
4. Moses speaks regarding blessings and curses— Deuteronomy 27:1–28:68
5. Moses' third speech with warnings and encouragement—Deuteronomy 29:1–30:20
6. Commissioning of Joshua and Moses' final words—Deuteronomy 31:1–34:12

God is not someone who gives up quickly on His children. God is patient and long-suffering. God demonstrated this through the many times He allowed His children to return to Him.

In the book of Numbers, God made a call to His children. He's making another call. *Ring! Ring! Ring! Ring!* Deuteronomy reveals how God is still calling His children to come back to Him. They were about to move into the

Promised Land after having forty years to think about how they allowed their fears to paralyze them. Disobedience created their current situation. Let's see what happened in the book of Deuteronomy.

Deuteronomy means "second law." After spending forty years in the wilderness and failing to obey, God wanted Moses to give the people final instructions before entering Canaan, the Promised Land. Moses also reminded them of all the history they experienced for the past four decades since leaving Egypt. The people looked for ways to overcome their fear during their forty years of wandering. Moses reminded the people of their history, God's law, and the Ten Commandments. Moses wanted them to learn from their past mistakes and rebuild their faith. He also gave them instructions on overcoming their fears of the situations they would find themselves facing in the future. The final chapters of Deuteronomy talk about Joshua's appointment as the new leader following Moses' death.

I once saw a triathlon shirt that read, "Eat-Train-Sleep-Repeat," and had an athletic logo for exercising. This is what you do every day, whether it's godly or ungodly. You cannot keep repeating the same behaviors over and over, expecting different outcomes. If you are wanting different outcomes for your life, they come from making different choices.

Do you have a broken heart or a crushed spirit? Do you worry about your past failures? If you do, it's okay. The same God who helped the Israelites rebuild their lives is the same God who is gladly willing to help you recover your life's worth. He's also aware of any past abuse and injustice inflicted on you by others. Here are some very comforting and profound thoughts that have helped me immensely. Before God created me, He knew every misdeed, every mistake, every lie, every betrayal, every thought, every sin that I would commit. Yet He still created me! Why? So that He could help me. You're unique to God, just like I am. We are all one of a kind, a designer's model, created for humanity's good. When God created you, He broke the mold. Remember, there will never be another you. So be your unique self for God.

Rebuilding brokenness is God's business; giving it to God is your business.

Can you hide from your past mistakes? Were the children of Israel able to hide from their past mistakes? Nope! While past mistakes are not desired, they are valuable to you and God for rebuilding your life. As a matter of fact, it is impossible to rebuild a powerful life with God without embracing and accepting your past sinful failures.

I used to allow what I thought others might be saying or thinking about me to paralyze me. Thoughts like these caused me to wander around in the wilderness of my mind. It was very ungodly, unhealthy, and toxic to me. To change and move away from this thought process, I had to allow God to reshape my thinking.

I can remember a turning point in my life many years ago. I sat down with God and my broken heart and wrote this to myself: People are going to believe what they want to believe. People are going to say what they want to say. People are going to do what they want to do. People are what they believe, say, and do. I cannot change that!

You see, God provided me with an exit plan to lead me out of my mind's wilderness. I was blessed to live in the land He promised where there is freedom. Satan operates wilderness living. I can only do three things for people who choose wilderness living: pray for them, encourage them, and be an example for them. If I do anything, either more or less, I would be practicing my old, past behaviors that caused me to be spiritually sick and stuck in the wilderness.

As Moses gave his three farewell speeches before he died, he reminded the people of God's boundaries to keep them safe. Moses' challenge to them was strong and firm because he knew God was serious about His words. You see, even Moses did not escape paying the price for disobedience. Because of Moses' disobedience, he could not enter the Promised Land. God used Moses as an example that we should learn from today. God means what He says!

My Verse for Golden Nuggets

> And now, Israel, what does the Lord your God ask of you but to fear the Lord your God, to walk in obedience to him, to love him, to serve the Lord your God with all your heart and with all your soul. (Deuteronomy 10:12)

Practical Applications for Your Life Today

- God always gives you instructions to prepare you and to protect you.
- You may think you're moving forward in life. However, in reality, you may still be wandering

around in your wilderness. Remember, the devil is the master deceiver.

- Moment by moment, remain focused on God's instructions, for your daily life.
- How many years has God given you to follow His instructions?
- Embrace God's instructions, for your very soul depends on them.
- When you genuinely seek God's love, you will become motivated to follow His instructions.

In fact, this is love for God: to keep his commands. And his commands are not burdensome. (1 John 5:3)

You will seek me and find me when you seek me with all your heart. (Jeremiah 29:13)

Prayer

Dear Heavenly Father, thank You for the reminders You give me. In this busy world, it is easy to lose focus on what You have in store for me. Please help me continually remind myself that my purpose in life is to honor, respect, and live for You. I believe that I will find You as I seek to do Your will. In Jesus' name, I pray. Amen.

*****

Wow! What an interesting sailing journey this has been thus far. We began with Genesis and ended with Deuteronomy. Let's take a moment to reflect on our past voyage thus far.

Remember the combination 5-12-5-5-12?

The five Books of Moses have been an eye-opener containing exciting stories and valuable lessons to help you on your daily journey with God.

Before we proceed into the second category, the twelve history books of the Old Testament, let's do a quick recap.

Genesis—This is where everything began.

Exodus—Moses leads the children of Israel out of slavery.

Leviticus—God knows the importance of laws in society, so He gave Moses the first set of requirements to be followed.

Numbers—The children of Israel spent forty years wandering in the wilderness. God also called for a head count.

Deuteronomy—God shows them mercy and provides them with yet another set of laws.

I hope you have learned that God is always there for His people, and that includes you. No matter how far you have drifted away from God, His hand is still there for you to grab.

Remember to keep moving forward in reading this book entirely. Now prepare yourself for twelve amazing books detailing God's people's history, our spiritual and physical ancestors. Sails up! All eyes on the page, all minds and hearts open. Someone pull up the anchor and let's set sail. I should tell you that there will be some major wars and battles on this voyage. Every great army needs a great military leader. Let's see if we can find one.

HISTORY OF

ISRAEL

JOSHUA

Outline of the Book of Joshua

1. Joshua's assignment—Joshua 1:1–18
2. Rahab helps the spies—Joshua 2:1–24
3. The people cross the Jordan River—Joshua 3:1–4:24
4. Circumcision and a visit by an angel—Joshua 5:1–15
5. Battle of Jericho—Joshua 6:1–27
6. Achan's sin brings death—Joshua 7:1–26
7. Renewed Israel defeats Ai—Joshua 8:1–35
8. Gibeon's trick—Joshua 9:1–27
9. Defending Gibeon and defeating the southern kings—Joshua 10:1–43
10. Capturing the north and a list of kings—Joshua 11:1–12:24
11. Dividing the land—Joshua 13:1–33
12. Land west of the Jordan—Joshua 14:1–19:51
13. More allotments and justice at last—Joshua 20:1–21:45
14. Eastern tribes praise God—Joshua 22:1–34
15. Joshua warns the people to stay faithful—Joshua 23:1–16
16. Covenant at Shechem and Joshua's death—Joshua 24:1–33

When was the last time you went into a battle to fight a war? My prayer is that many of you can say never; however, battles are going on in your life daily.

That being said, the next question is, who is fighting your battles? It is better to have someone else fight your battles for you. You need someone who knows the enemy's tactics, deceptions, tricks, and lies. You ultimately need someone who knows how to help you become victorious.

Here is where Joshua comes in. You'll find that God used Joshua while fighting His battles for Him. Would you like God to fight your battles? People, places, and situations are no match for God. Let's march forward with God's military man, Captain Joshua.

The second phase of an exciting journey of understanding the Old Testament will now begin.

When some of you embarked on this learning journey through the Old Testament, there were probably conflicting thoughts in your head. However, you followed the thought that told you it was possible to increase your knowledge. Those thoughts could be likened to those of Joshua and Caleb, encouraging them to keep their faith in God's abilities.

Many times, when confronted with challenges, all we need to conquer is a willingness to listen. Yes, there may be thousands of other conflicting voices, but are they the voice of God? In the end, we always have a reward for obedience, and the same is true for Joshua. Let's see how far listening to God's voice would take Joshua and the Israelites into the Promised Land.

God appointed Joshua to lead the people after the death of Moses. This book tells how God helped Joshua and the Israelites conquer and take over the Promised Land occupied by the Canaanites. (Canaanites were known for worshipping idols.) During much of Moses' life, Joshua worked closely with him until he died. Being that close to a great leader like Moses gave Joshua the skills to lead the people of Israel. After seeing miraculous victories over their enemies and crossing the Jordan River and conquering Jericho's mighty city, the Israelites continued to obey God. In return, God did great things on their behalf.

Before his death, Joshua reminded the people of God's promise to them. He also said this,

> But if serving the LORD seems undesirable to you, then choose for yourselves this day whom you will serve, whether the gods your ancestors served beyond the Euphrates, or the gods of the Amorites, in whose land you are living. But as for me and my household, we will serve the LORD. (Joshua 24:15)

My Verse for Golden Nuggets

> Have I not commanded you? Be strong and courageous. Do not be afraid; do not be discouraged, for the Lord your

God will be with you wherever you go. (Joshua 1:9)

Practical Applications for Your Life Today

- Your daily thoughts, words, and actions dictate who you are.
- How would you feel if God spoke these words to you, "Be strong and courageous"?
- God wants to be first in every aspect of your life. He's eager to assist you.
- When you place God in your battles, you will always have victories.
- Victories daily or defeat daily? It's your choice.
- Your army versus God's army?
- You can march with encouragement or retreat in discouragement.
- Who leads and fights your daily battles?
- Do you only need God in your big battles, your little battles, or both?

Prayer

Heavenly Father, every day, there are so many battles and wars going on in my mind. It gets confusing and very discouraging because, at times, I feel defeated. Help me, God, to have the confidence Joshua had to march daily by following Your guidance. I need You in every daily situation that I encounter. In Jesus' name, I pray. Amen.

When Joshua died, the children of Israel faced a dilemma. If their faith were only in Joshua and his leadership, their faith would die with Joshua. But if their faith was in God, they would move forward with God. Let's see what happens.

JUDGES

Outline of the Book of Judges

1. Failure to drive out all the Canaanites—Judges 1:1–3:6
2. Othniel—Judges 3:7–11
3. Ehud and Shamgar—Judges 3:12–31
4. Deborah and Barak—Judges 4:1–5:31
5. Gideon, Tola, and Jair—Judges 6:1–10:5
6. Jephthah, Ibzan, Elon, Abdon—Judges 10:6–12:15
7. Samson—Judges 13:1–16:31
8. Abandoning the true God—Judges 17:1–18:31
9. Moral wickedness, civil war, and its consequences—Judges 19:1–21:25

Many reality shows today feature judges presiding over minor offenses. In these reality shows, the judge's main objective is to administer justice, usually between two warring parties. Although this book is called Judges, you will find that these were different kinds of judges. Let us meet some of these judges that God appointed to aid the children of Israel.

The book of Judges covers the period from the death of Joshua to the birth of Samuel. However, this book's

44

central message is that God will never allow sin to go unpunished. It was clear that Israel was God's chosen people. God's marching orders were made very clear in how they were to deal with the sinful Canaanites currently living in the land promised to them by God. However, due to their weakness and inability to resist Canaanite influences, the Israelites frequently engaged in blatant immorality and followed after their gods.

Strong leadership was lacking, and the Israelites continued to struggle with a constant rebellion and sin cycle. "In those days, Israel had no king, so everyone did as they saw fit." The Israelites followed a pattern of falling into sin, which led them to be enslaved, then they would cry out to God for help. Each time the people cried out for help, God would eventually send a leader known as a judge. This cycle happened about fifteen times.

Because of God's love for them, He heard their cries and raised leaders to deliver them. Some of the judges I can identify with are Gideon, Samson, and Jephthah. Gideon had feelings of inadequacy, Samson had problems with lust and pride, and Jephthah suffered ridicule while he was growing up. Later in life, God powerfully used Jephthah. He learned to forgive and committed himself and his daughter fully to the Lord through his journey, no matter the cost. Wow!

My Verses for Golden Nuggets

Then, the Israelites did evil in the eyes of the LORD and served the Baals. They forsook the LORD, the God of their ancestors, who had brought them out of Egypt. They followed and worshiped various gods of the peoples around them. They aroused the LORD's anger because they forsook him and served Baal and the Ashtoreths. (Judges 2:11–13)

Therefore, the LORD was very angry with Israel and said, "Because this nation has violated the covenant I ordained for their ancestors and has not listened to me, I will no longer drive out before them any of the nations Joshua left when he died. I will use them to test Israel and see whether they will keep the way of the LORD and walk in it as their ancestors did." The LORD had allowed those nations to remain; he did not drive them out at once by giving them into the hands of Joshua. (Judges 2:20–23)

In those days, Israel had no king; everyone did as they saw fit. (Judges 17:6)

Practical Applications for Your Life Today

- God always hears your cry. Do you follow His answers and solutions?

- God wants to shower your life with love, kindness, and mercy.
- Got fear? Get God! Been ridiculed? Let God raise you to a higher calling. Got lust? Get closer to God's love to fulfill what's empty inside of you.
- Sin will always victimize you.
- Godly sorrow always gets God's attention, not just being sorry that you got caught.
- You want to work with God daily and focus on asking Him for help with your words, thoughts, and actions. Neglecting to do so will increase your darkness and distance between you and God.
- Have you ever felt inadequate, ridiculed, or some other negative emotion? If so, build a bridge to get over it with God.
- Remembering what happened in the past should provide you with crucial lessons on how to conduct yourself in the present.
- Do you feel as if God is disciplining you right now?
- Do you know that He disciplines those He loves? (Hebrews 12:5–11)

Prayer

Dear Heavenly Father, I am so thankful that You are a kind and merciful God. Please hear my prayers and my cries as I seek to live for You. I know that I have provoked You with my thoughts, words, and actions. I have many things that only You can help me with, such as fear, loneliness, lust, pride, anger, and other things that make me feel inadequate. I believe in You and Your power. Thank You for being the ultimate helper and judge. In Jesus' name, I pray. Amen.

RUTH

Outline of the Book of Ruth

1. Ruth returns to Judah from Moab with Naomi—Ruth 1:1–22
2. Ruth gleans grain in Boaz's field—Ruth 2:1–23
3. Following Jewish customs, Ruth lets Boaz know he is a kinsman-redeemer and that she is eligible to marry him—Ruth 3:1–18
4. Boaz marries Ruth, and together, they cared for Naomi. Ruth and Boaz have a son who becomes an ancestor of Jesus, the Messiah—Ruth 4:1–22

Have you ever lost a loved one? Have you ever been so heartbroken that you just wanted to die? Have you ever been so extremely sad that the joyfulness of others made you even more depressed? Have you ever lost a spouse and buried two children? This is what happened to Naomi. The loss of a loved one can be devastating, and it always seems premature.

There are times we find ourselves in situations in which we think all hope is gone. We live in a world of uncertainty where it seems that disaster can strike at any time. We may sometimes wonder, does God indeed have a plan for our lives?

I choose to call the book of Ruth "the book of hope" because just when the devil thinks he is winning and all hope seems lost, God is always there to have the last say. "What, then, shall we say in response to these things? If God is for us, who can be against us?" (Romans 8:31)

Ruth's story begins with a famine in Israel. Because of this lack of food, a man from Israel named Elimelech, his wife, Naomi, and two sons moved from Israel to Moab. Elimelech died in Moab, and Naomi's two sons married Moabite women, Ruth and Orpah. Soon Naomi's two sons also died, and the three widows were left alone.

Naomi decided to move back to Israel. Ruth and Orpah said they would accompany her, but Naomi urged them to return home. Orpah went back to her father's house, but Ruth vowed to stay with Naomi and return to Israel with her. Ruth spoke these powerful words to Naomi, her mother-in-law, "Where you go I will go, and where you stay I will stay. Your people will be my people and your God my God" (Ruth 1:16).

Ruth and Naomi returned to Israel and were poverty-stricken. The law required property owners to leave some grain in the field for the poor and widows, such as Naomi and Ruth (Leviticus 23:22). Ruth provided for herself and Naomi by gathering the leftover grain in the fields of a wealthy landowner named Boaz. Boaz was a relative of Naomi. Naomi urged Ruth to go and ask Boaz for help. Boaz married Ruth. They became the great-grandparents of King David, from whose lineage Jesus came. (Are you still following the bloodline?)

The genealogy of Jesus cannot be complete without mentioning Ruth's name. Keep in mind that our first parents were Adam and Eve. We are all a part of their genealogy that continues to this day. It's essential to keep this spiritual genealogy and bloodline going and growing until Jesus returns.

My Verses for Golden Nuggets

But Ruth replied, "Don't urge me to leave you or to turn back from you. Where you go I will go, and where you stay I will stay. Your people will be my people and your God my God. Where you die I will die, and there I will be buried. May the Lord deal with me, be it ever so severely, if even death separates you and me." (Ruth 1:16–17)

Practical Applications for Your Life Today

- Pain, suffering, and confusion will come your way. When it does, who are you going to trust?
- Remember the *one* who can turn your sadness into joy and give you a "crown of beauty instead of ashes" (Isaiah 61:3).
- Holding onto your self-will conflicts with God's will for your life.

- You can never fail so long as God is on your side.
- Your decisions and actions today affect not only this generation but generations to come.

Prayer

Dear Heavenly Father, please help me to trust You no matter what is happening. Help my heart know that Your timing is always perfect and that You will place the right people in my path for Your goodness. You alone can provide me the necessary strength to increase my commitment and devotion toward You. In Jesus' name, I pray. Amen!

*****

Before we go through the remaining books, I have created a helpful reference guide with information that will help you from getting confused. This information is something that I wish I had many years ago. I hope that you find this guide helpful, and you will refer to it as you continue to read.

The nation of Israel was united with one earthly king to lead them. Here are the first three kings:

King Saul
King David
King Solomon

The kingdom was divided under King Rehoboam, Solomon's son:

Kingdom:	Israel	Judah
Location:	North	South
King:	Jeroboam	Rehoboam
City:	Samaria	Jerusalem (Temple)

The northern kingdom, referred to as Israel, and the southern kingdom, Judah.

1 SAMUEL

Outline of the Book of 1 Samuel

1. Samuel's rise, the capture of the ark of the covenant, and Samuel's work as a judge—1 Samuel 1:1–7:17.
2. The people of Israel demand a king—1 Samuel 8:1–22.
3. Saul becomes king and battles Israel's enemies. God rejects Saul after he disobeys the Lord—1 Samuel 9:1–15:35
4. David is anointed king, defeats Goliath, befriends Jonathan, and flees from Saul—1 Samuel 16:1–30:30
5. Saul and his sons die in battle—1 Samuel 31:1–13

News flash—riots are going on all around the United States and different countries, and the leaders are at a loss as to how to handle these situations.

Today protests are ongoing, even amidst a global pandemic. Protesters around the world are calling for police reform and an end to racism.

Several cities have imposed curfews and boarded up businesses following accounts of looting.

Headline news—the coronavirus is spreading through-out the world.

There is so much bad news going on all around the world today. Where does it all come from? This is what God's Word has to say, "What causes fights and quarrels among you? Don't they come from your desires that battle within you? You want something but don't get it. You kill and covet, but you cannot have what you want" (James 4:1).

All over the world, many people are suffering because of leaders who lack integrity. Even in some families, a lack of integrity has caused parents to abandon their respon-sibilities of raising godly children. In fact, when you look around, you see a world filled with lies, hypocrisy, and deception. The same is true in the times of Samuel.

This book starts by telling us about Hannah, the mother of Samuel. Hannah had no children; however, her husband's second wife did. The second wife made fun of Hannah for being unable to bear children. This hurt Hannah, and in her pain, she shed many tears. This is the beginning of what turns into a beautiful story about the commitment Hannah made to the Lord.

One time, Hannah was in the temple crying her heart out to the Lord. Hannah made a promise to the Lord that if she was gifted with a child, she would dedicate her child to being raised in the temple. Hannah gave birth to Samuel. When Samuel was a small child, Hannah dedicated him to being raised in the temple by Eli the priest.

While in the temple, Eli's sons were committing sinful acts such as lying, cheating, stealing, and having sinful relationships with women. You will see that Eli never bothered to correct his two sons for their blatant disrespect toward God. It may take time for some sinful consequences to be revealed. However, God is not going to let unconfessed sins go unpunished.

One night while Samuel was sleeping in the temple, God spoke to him. Samuel's response was, "Speak, Lord, your servant is listening." God informed Samuel that Eli and both of his sons would die on the same day. This information was difficult for Samuel to share with Eli. What God revealed to Samuel came true. Eli and his sons died on the same day. Samuel stayed dedicated to God, and his impact was so powerful that he led the Israelites back to a faithful relationship with God.

Near the end of Samuel's life, God appointed Saul as king over Israel because they complained that they wanted a king like all the other nations. God wasn't happy with their request, but He gave them a king anyway. Sadly, Saul soon rebelled against God. This rebellion caused God to reject Saul as king and choose another king to take his place. God told Samuel to anoint David to lead the Israelites in Saul's place while Saul was still on the throne.

Before becoming king, David won many battles for Israel. The most well-known is the defeat of Goliath. Saul came to view David's popularity and military skill as a threat. He was full of rage and jealousy and made several attempts on David's life. Rather than fight back, David went into hiding. David and those loyal to him fled from Saul's pursuit for several years.

Eventually, the Philistines came to fight against the Israelites again. During this great battle, Saul was wounded, and his three sons were killed. The injured Saul fell on his sword to kill himself rather than let the Philistines take him captive. Saul's downfall came about because of pride, lust, disobedience, jealousy, and bitterness. Faithfulness and forgiveness allowed David to succeed.

My Verse for Golden Nuggets

> David was greatly distressed because the men were talking of stoning him; each one was bitter in spirit because of his sons and daughters. But David found strength in the Lord his God. (1 Samuel 30:6)

I love this verse.

Practical Applications for Your Life Today

- There will always be those who will accuse you of wrongful things. Let God be your judge and equalizer.
- Every day you are in training! Who is your trainer? You? Satan? Or God?
- To be successful in life, you must be willing to ask for God's help to fight your battles.
- When God speaks to you through His Word, it is not a suggestion but rather instructions to be followed for your protection and well-being.

- The secret place of peace is found in the presence of God.
- Be careful what you ask for and who you follow. Israel asked for a king. What followed was a downfall due to poor leadership. There is only one true King.
- Do you have any weaknesses in your life, such as pride, disobedience, jealousy, and bitterness? You can begin a new life through Jesus. To qualify for His help, you must be willing to humble yourself and follow His teachings.

Prayer

Dear Heavenly Father, being devoted to You is what my heart desires. However, at times, my heart can become like Saul's and others who have rejected You. So please, Father, I pray for a change of heart, attitude, and behaviors to show that I want to honor You. In Jesus' name, I pray. Amen.

2 SAMUEL

Outline of the Book of 2 Samuel

1. David becomes king of Judah and Israel—1:1–7:29
2. David conquers Israel's enemies—8:1–10:19
3. David sins with Bathsheba and has her husband, Uriah, killed—11:1–12:23
4. Bathsheba gives birth to Solomon—12:24–31
5. Amnon, son of David, rapes his half-sister Tamar—13:1–22
6. Absalom, David's son, kills Amnon and returns to Jerusalem—13:23–14:33
7. Absalom rebels against his father and is killed—15:1–20:26
8. David praises God; exploits of David's mighty men—21:1–24:25

No one really knows when they are going to die. However, it is a known fact that death is 100 percent unavoidable. "And just as it is appointed for man to die once, and after that comes judgment" (Hebrews 9:27 ESV).

Second Samuel starts with Saul's death and tells of King David's forty-year reign. As king, David managed the affairs of the kingdom well. Unfortunately, he did not do so well with his personal life. After David committed murder and adultery, God sent the prophet Nathan to confront David about his sinful actions. What Nathan said and how he presented God's chastisement grieved David to the depths of his soul. After this rebuke, David's heart revealed a genuine change of attitude and action. God then used David in a mighty way to lead the nation of Israel, with plans to build a temple for God. David continued to follow God. He looked to God for his forgiveness, strength, and guidance.

Despite all of David's sinful actions, when he confessed his sins and changed his behaviors, God referred to David as a man after his own heart (1 Samuel 13:14). Beautiful!

My Verse for Golden Nuggets

> Then David said to Nathan, "I have sinned against the Lord." (2 Samuel 12:13)

Practical Applications for Your Life Today:

- Regardless of your sins, you can become a person after God's own heart.
- When you have a heart of repentance and forgiveness, you receive God's favor.
- God uses imperfect people like you to accomplish His perfect will.
- Do you realize that God has given you more than a sufficient amount of grace for your failures? Are

you reaching for His forgiveness or going in the opposite direction?

- Why not make the rest of your life the best of your life?
- Do you have any Nathans in your life who will challenge you about ungodly behaviors?
- Accountably is not optional when living for God.

Prayer

Dear Heavenly Father, I can relate to David's times of lust, dishonesty, and deception. My sins have a direct impact on my life and those closest to me. Please help me, Lord, to put my life in order so that I can become a person after Your own heart. In Jesus' mighty name, I pray. Amen.

1 KINGS

Outline of the Book of 1 Kings

1. David's death and Solomon's ascent as king—1 Kings 1:1–2:46
2. Solomon's wisdom and government—1 Kings 3:1–4:34
3. Building the temple and palace—1 Kings 5:1–8:66
4. Solomon's wives and his downfall—1 Kings 9:1–12:43
5. Northern tribes revolt—1 Kings 12:1–33
6. Deeds of kings of Israel and Judah—1 Kings 13:1–16:34
7. Ministry of Elijah—1 Kings 17:1–21:29
8. Kings of Israel and Judah and Ahab's death—1 Kings 22:1–53

Why do we go to school? Why do we read books and attend seminars and lectures? Why is there always a push for people to obtain a higher education? Of course, the answer would be to gain wisdom, knowledge, and understanding. In the book of 1 Kings, you will find out whose wisdom and knowledge are superior. You will learn from the wisest man who ever lived. Besides learning about the king's lavish lifestyle, this book also has some living pearls of wisdom that can help you make wise choices in your daily decisions.

Every day you encounter numerous intersections in your life. By intersections, I mean choices. I don't know about you, but I'm thankful that God has given me today to gain more wisdom to better my life for Him. Let's see what kind of knowledge we can gain from the first book of Kings.

This book covers Israel's history, from the last days of King David to the death of wicked King Ahab. After David's reign, his son Solomon became king. Solomon was best known for his wisdom. After Solomon's death, his son Rehoboam took over. While Solomon was wise, Rehoboam was foolish. Rehoboam refused to listen to the older men's wise counsel, and he accepted the advice from his friends. His friends encouraged Rehoboam to make the Israelites' lives more difficult. This choice caused the twelve tribes of Israel to divide. Ten of the tribes formed the northern kingdom of Israel. The other two tribes formed the southern kingdom of Judah.

After the division, Israel in the north never had a king who was faithful to God. However, Judah had some good kings who put an end to idol worship and encouraged them to change their behaviors. This book describes each king as being either faithful or wicked. When they were faithful, God gave them peace in the land. When they disobeyed, they suffered negative consequences for their choices. God desires to have a close relationship with all His children. Even though God warned them about how a king would mistreat them, they rejected God and wanted a king any-way. It is beautiful how God responds with love even after being rejected by His people.

My Verses for Golden Nuggets

> God gave Solomon wisdom and very great insight, and a breadth of under-standing as measureless as the sand on the seashore. Solomon's wisdom was greater than the wisdom of all the people of the East, and greater than all the wisdom of Egypt... And his fame spread to all the surrounding nations. (1 Kings 4:29–31)

Practical Applications for Your Life Today

- Have you ever rejected God by your words and actions?
- Have you seen how God's love for you is unconditional?
- Do you know that God has an abundance of wis-dom to give you?
- Have you ever prayed for wisdom above anything else?
- When was the last time you conducted an honest, godly assessment of all areas in your life?
- Ask God to reveal the areas in your life that are hindering you.

- Unchecked pride guarantees you a life of distraction, defeat, and destruction.
- Do you realize that your current circumstances are directly related to your past and present choices?
- Have you chosen Jesus as your ultimate King to lead you?

Prayer

Dear Heavenly Father, I need Your wisdom and insight to navigate Satan's numerous traps surrounding me. Lord, I have allowed multiple distractions to keep me from putting You first in my daily life. Only You, Father, can help me with Your guiding and gentle hand of love. In Jesus' name, I pray. Amen.

2 KINGS

Outline of the Book of 2 Kings

1. Elisha's ministry—2 Kings 1:1–8:29
2. The actions of the kings of Israel and Judah—2 Kings 9:1–16:20
3. Israel destroyed and exiled to Assyria—2 Kings 17:41
4. Reigns of the kings of Judah—2 Kings 18:1–23:37
5. Judah is destroyed and taken captive to Babylon—2 Kings 24:1–25:30

This book picks up after the death of the evil King Ahab. Israel has already been divided between the north and the south. It continues until the fall of both Israel and Judah. Because of the Israelites' sin, God allowed foreign nations to overthrow both kingdoms. God's people suffered from denial and unbelief, which led to their spiritual deterioration. They allowed sin to become their normal way of life.

God sent prophets such as Elijah, Elisha, and Isaiah to advise godly kings on how to restore the Israelites. Though there were various periods of change and renewal, the people eventually went back to being self-centered and worshiped idols. This toxic environment kept them in a continual state of disobedience to God. They were disrespectful to the Lord in many ways, especially in the area of sexual sins (which is common in our society today). However, the God who will not allow unrepentant sin to go unpunished allowed the Assyrians to capture Israel and the Babylonians to capture Judah. The Babylonians destroyed the beautiful temple that Solomon had built and carried the people of Judah into captivity. But God promised that one day there would be a day of restoration. God believed in His people. However, they needed to experience the consequences of their disobedient choices. Are you thankful that God is willing to forgive?

My Verses for Golden Nuggets

> So the Lord was very angry with Israel and removed them from his presence. Only the tribe of Judah was left, and even Judah did not keep the commands of the Lord their God. They followed the practices Israel had introduced. Therefore, the Lord rejected all the people of Israel; he afflicted them and gave them into the hands of plunderers until he thrust them from his presence. (2 Kings 17:18–20)

Practical Applications for Your Life Today

- Allowing sin to go unchecked is very destructive, both to you and those around you.

- Is God a significant influence in your life today? Don't be your own leader.
- If living a godly life was easy, then the world would be filled with God-fearing people.
- Did you know that only courageous people live for God?
- Acknowledge your struggles with sin, seek godly counsel, and stay accountable to someone.
- A self-reliant and self-centered person leaves no room for God in their life.
- Living for God gives you unlimited access to spiritual artillery to help you to combat sin.
- How free your life will be once you allow God to change you from the inside out.
- Have you ever imagined your life free from habitual sin? Remember, "*all* things are possible with God."
- You can become a lighthouse for others leading them to the pathway of God.
- More God-seeking people are needed; if interested, please apply from within.

Prayer

Dear Heavenly Father, the world is filled with negative influences and people who are not living to please You. I have been guilty of not following You to the best of my abilities. Please forgive me. In spite of my sinful past behaviors, I can still be a lighthouse for You. Please help me to do what needs to be done. In Jesus' name, I pray. Amen.

1 CHRONICLES

Outline of the Book of 1 Chronicles

1. The genealogies of Israel—1 Chronicles 1:1–9:44
2. Saul commits suicide—1 Chronicles 10:1–14
3. David becomes king over all Israel—1 Chronicles 11:1–12:40
4. David brings the ark of the covenant to Jerusalem—1 Chronicles 13:1–16:43
5. God makes a covenant with David—1 Chronicles 17:1–27
6. David's military actions—1 Chronicles 18:1–21:30
7. David prepares to build the temple—1 Chronicles 22:1–29:20
8. Solomon becomes king; David dies—1 Chronicles 29:21–30

If someone asked you to write a book on your genealogy, could you do it? How many generations could you recall? Ezra, the author of 1 and 2 Chronicles, takes us on a long journey, detailing how it all began with Adam to the various conquests of the kings.

Some may be tempted to skip both books of Chronicles, thinking most of the accounts have already been covered in the books of Kings. But the truth remains, just like watching a classic movie and its remake, essential differences are always there. These two books deliver a new message, a new tone, about God's consistent love and involvement with His children. These books also fill in missing details from 1 and 2 Kings.

First Chronicles shows that God is always faithful to His covenant. While 1 and 2 Chronicles cover the same period as 2 Samuel and 1 and 2 Kings, Chronicles is written from a different point of view. These two books were written to help the people to rebuild their hope in the faithfulness of God. After being held in captivity by the Babylonians, the exiles are finally allowed to return to Israel. The first book of Chronicles opens with a genealogy that begins with Adam and ends with the first group of exiles returning to their homeland. Chronicles' accurate coverage of this rich history could only have been made possible by a magnificent God.

After the genealogy, we read about the death of King Saul and the beginning of David's reign. David led the people to worship God, but he was not allowed to build the temple. This privilege was reserved for his son, Solomon. God also promised David that one of his descendants would sit on the throne forever. Eventually, Jesus fulfilled this promise.

My Verse for Golden Nuggets

Jabez cried out to the God of Israel,
"Oh, that you would bless me and enlarge

my territory! Let your hand be with me and keep me from harm so that I will be free from pain." And God granted his request. (1 Chronicles 4:10)

David said to Gad, "I am in deep distress. Let me fall into the hands of the LORD, for his mercy is very great; but do not let me fall into the hands of men." (1 Chronicles 21:13)

Practical Applications for Your Life Today:

- Do you realize that your life is a part of God's continuous story? What is being written about your life?
- God is in the business of building and rebuilding lives.
- No matter how far from God you find yourself, you can always retrace your steps back to Him.
- God will erase all your sins forever.
- Pay attention! Every opportunity gives you a chance to make a difference in the world. "If I cannot do great things, I can do small things in a great way" (Martin Luther King Jr.).
- Grade yourself with an honest assessment of your daily situations with either a pass or fail—watch how you will grow spiritually.

- God knows your thoughts. "For the LORD searches every heart and understands every desire and every thought" (1 Chronicles 28:9).
- Seek to be a God pleaser in your heart instead of a people pleaser in your flesh.

Prayer

Dear Heavenly Father, as I sit here thinking of how blessed I am to read the true stories of Your love, especially Your patience for humanity, I am in awe! I praise you, Lord, that my story is still being written. There are areas of my life that need to be revised for Your glory. Please help me to do this. In Jesus' name, I pray. Amen.

2 CHRONICLES

Outline of the Book of 2 Chronicles

1. Solomon prepares, builds, and dedicates the temple—2 Chronicles 1:1–7:22
2. Solomon's achievements and fame—2 Chronicles 8:1–9:31
3. Reign of Rehoboam, Solomon's son—2 Chronicles 10:1–12:16
4. Reigns of good and wicked kings—2 Chronicles 13:1–36:16
5. Exile into Babylon—2 Chronicles 36:17–21
6. Restoration of God's people to Israel—2 Chronicles 36:22–23

Second Chronicles describes in great detail Solomon's achievement of building the temple in Jerusalem. Because of his faithfulness, God told Solomon he would be the wisest man who ever lived. Sadly, after his death, Solomon's son, Rehoboam, caused Israel's division into two kingdoms when he became king. Despite this mistake, David's descendants continued to reign over Judah's southern kingdom, just as God promised. Some of Judah's kings failed to live righteously, which led them to worship idols and rebel against God. Others succeeded in trying to get the people to turn away from sin and follow God. God granted renewal and restoration to the good kings, but many other kings were hard-hearted and led people back to their sinful ways. As a result, judgment came upon the people, and they were taken captive. Despite their sinfulness, 2 Chronicles ends with a positive note of grace. The last words of this book are King Cyrus' order that God would rebuild the temple and restore peace.

My Verses for Golden Nuggets

God said to Solomon, "Since this is your heart's desire and you have not asked for wealth, possessions or honor, nor for the death of your enemies, and since you have not asked for a long life but for wisdom and knowledge to govern my people over whom I have made you king, therefore wisdom and knowledge will be given you. And I will also give you wealth, possessions, and honor, such as no king who was before you ever had, and none after you will have." (2 Chronicles 1:11–12)

In everything that he undertook in the service of God's temple and in obedience to the law and the commands, he sought his God and worked wholeheartedly. And so he prospered. (2 Chronicles 31:21)

Practical Applications for Your Life Today

- "if my people, who are called by my name, will humble themselves and pray and seek my face and turn from their wicked ways, then I will hear from heaven, and I will forgive their sin and will heal their land." (2 Chronicles 7:14)
- Do you know when you pray the all-knowing God is listening?
- Because of your faithfulness, are you experiencing God's faithfulness?
- What are some of the things that may be blocking your spiritual blessings?
- What spiritual blessings are you experiencing in your heart this moment?
- Do you have the willingness to turn from your wicked ways?
- Your thoughts have an immediate impact on what you do next.

Prayer

Dear Heavenly Father, as Solomon prayed for wisdom and knowledge, I would like to pray for the same. I really need to deepen my relationship with You. Please forgive me for all my self-seeking ways and help me daily to surrender my pride. In Jesus' name, I pray. Amen.

EZRA

Judah After Captivity
(Ezra is listed as a history book.)

Outline of the Book of Ezra

1. King Cyrus permits Zerubbabel to lead the first group of exiles to their land and rebuild the temple—Ezra 1:1–2:70
2. Rebuilding the temple—Ezra 3:1–4:13
3. Opposition to the rebuilding—Ezra 4:1–24
4. Completion and dedication of the temple—Ezra 5:1–6:22
5. The return of Ezra's second group of exiles—Ezra 7:1–8:36
6. Ezra and the people deal with the problem of mixed marriages—Ezra 9:1–10:44

After watching an episode of one of your favorite shows or finishing a series, have you ever found yourself anxiously anticipating a new episode or a new book release? Then, when you learned that a new episode or new book was finally released, hopefully, you felt excited and wanted to continue what you started.

The book of Ezra and Nehemiah are similar in nature. They are a continuation of the books of Chronicles. When reading these books, you will feel like you are reading a continuing and exciting narrative.

Ezra's name means "help." He was a direct descendant of Aaron, the first high priest. Ezra was not only a priest, but he was also a scribe and a teacher. His zeal for God and his love for the word of God were inspiring and contagious. Ezra led a group of Jews out of captivity back to Israel. During this time, the Persian empire was in power. (Please keep in mind that the Persians conquered the Babylonian empire who initially took Judah into captivity.)

It's interesting to see how God moved the hearts of three nonreligious kings, Cyrus, Darius, and Artaxerxes, to encourage and help the Jewish people return home at the exact time promised by God. In this book, Ezra gives accounts of two returns from Babylon. A man named Zerubbabel led the first return, and the second occurred about sixty or so years later, led by Ezra. Zerubbabel focused on rebuilding the temple, while Ezra concentrated on restoring the spiritual condition of the people. Zerubbabel was a descendant of King David who served as governor of Judah. The people began rebuilding the temple and resumed animal sacrifices.

Some of the neighboring peoples offered to help rebuild the temple. They even went so far as to say, "We believe in your God." Fortunately, the Israelites were wise and told them, "No." Of course, this answer caused their neighbors to reveal their true colors. They went to extreme measures to force the Jews to stop work on the temple.

Almost twenty years later, King Darius of Persia finally permitted them to finish the task.

When Ezra returned, he was discouraged upon finding that the people had intermarried with foreign women. This sin was great in the sight of God. God had instructed the Israelites not to intermarry with the surrounding nations because of their worship of idols and false gods. When Ezra heard they had intermarried, he fell on his face and began weeping before the Lord. His crying was so intense it caused the Israelites to start weeping too. The Israelites repented and turned away from their sins. Ezra's message of hope encouraged people to rebuild their lives with God.

My Verses for Golden Nuggets

> For Ezra had devoted himself to the study and observance of the Law of the LORD, and to teaching its decrees and laws in Israel. (Ezra 7:10)

> Then the peoples around them set out to discourage Judah's people and make them afraid to go on building. They bribed officials to work against them and frustrate their plans during the entire reign of Cyrus king of Persia and down to the reign of Darius king of Persia. (Ezra 4:4–5)

While Ezra was praying and confessing, weeping, and throwing himself down before the house of God, a large crowd of Israelites—men, women, and children—gathered around him and began weeping bitterly. Then Shekaniah, the son of Jehiel, one of the descendants of Elam, said to Ezra, "We have been unfaithful to our God by marrying foreign women from the peoples around us. But despite this, there is still hope for Israel. Now let us make a covenant before our God to send away all these women and their children, in accordance with the counsel of my lord and of those who fear the commands of our God. Let it be done according to the Law. Rise up; this matter is in you." (Ezra 10:1–4)

Practical Applications for Your Life Today

- Does your life need some encouragement and rebuilding?
- Are there people, places, or things currently in your life that interfere with your work for the Lord?
- Even though you have not kept your commitments to God, His love never changes. He's waiting for you to change.

- Your disappointments and frustrations can be God's method of reshaping and conforming you to His glory.
- When God's children were given an open invitation to return to their homeland, some were too comfortable to leave. Are you too comfortable to make the needed changes in your life?
- When you decide to commit your life to God, please expect opposition.
- Opposition can come from friends, enemies, and even loved ones.
- Seek to be a God pleaser, not a people pleaser.

Prayer

Dearest Heavenly Father, I now can see You have always had people who were there to help those struggling. Even when people were once defiant toward You, with Your help, they were able to change. Father, I need to make changes so I can be all that You created me to be. Help me to be a light to others for Your glory, not mine. In Jesus' name, I pray. Amen!

NEHEMIAH

Judah After Captivity
(Nehemiah is listed as a history book.
However, it is written after captivity.)

Outline of the Book of Nehemiah

1. The preparation to reconstruct the wall—
    Nehemiah 1:1–2:20
2. The dangers that occurred with the reconstruction
    to finish the wall—Nehemiah 3:1–7:3
3. Nehemiah registers the people who returned from
    exile—Nehemiah 7:4–73
4. Ezra reads the Law, and the people renew their
    covenant—Nehemiah 8:1–10:39
5. The people occupying Jerusalem are listed—
    Nehemiah 11:1–12:43
6. Nehemiah cleans up civil and religious offenses—
    Nehemiah 12:44–13:31

To be healthy in life, one must learn the importance of setting up healthy emotional, physical, and spiritual boundaries. When people have no boundaries, they open themselves up for countless violations from people who will readily take advantage of them and exploit them. Boundaries are not something that takes away freedom. They are for protecting your freedom.

This is why Nehemiah's work and leadership were so critical to rebuilding the walls. The altar, foundation, and the temple had been completed in Jerusalem. However, the city had no walls or gates to safely protect God's people from being invaded and facing their enemies' violations. God is always in the building, rebuilding, reconciling, and reconstruction business. Are you ready to build some walls of protection in your life?

The book of Nehemiah continues the story of the Jews returning from exile. Nehemiah returned to Jerusalem about thirteen years after Ezra. He was in Babylon when he received the devastating news that Jerusalem's walls had been destroyed during the Babylonian invasion. When he heard this, Nehemiah literally sat down and wept. While the temple was rebuilt, the walls were still piles of rubble, and the city was defenseless.

Nehemiah gave up his high position as a cupbearer to King Artaxerxes of Persia and became the governor of Jerusalem. The walls were weak, and the gates had been burned, making Jerusalem vulnerable to raids and harassment by intruders. Nehemiah led the people to rebuild the walls of Jerusalem.

This was not an easy undertaking. Nehemiah and the Israelites faced some serious opposition from their enemies. The enemies of God worked tirelessly to trick and trap Nehemiah. They even told slanderous lies and threatened him with violence. Despite all of this, Nehemiah and

God's people were not deterred from building and finishing the project.

They refused to waste their time getting caught up in all the drama, lies, and deceptions by the haters. It is powerful to see how Nehemiah confronted each situation head-on. Some of his friends encouraged him to run and hide. Instead, with God's guidance, he took the necessary precautions by having men strategically placed in key places on the wall at night. During the day, men worked with one hand while having their sword ready to fight in the other hand. Dedication to God and hard work always bring about godly outcomes. Amazingly, the entire wall was completed in only fifty-two days.

Through Nehemiah's leadership, he was able to help the people in Jerusalem come together for the greater good of the community. He brought political reform and worked with Ezra to bring spiritual reform to God's people. God used Ezra, Nehemiah, and others who were willing to help when they saw a need. Being used by God to help fulfill needs in the world is a fantastic way to live.

My Verse for Golden Nuggets

So the wall was completed on the twenty-fifth of Elul, in fifty-two days. When all our enemies heard about this, all the surrounding nations were afraid and lost their self-confidence, because they realized that this work had been done with the help of our God. (Nehemiah 6:15–16)

Practical Applications for Your Life Today

- On a scale from 1–10, how would you rate your emotional, physical, and spiritual boundaries?
- You are facing daily attacks on your life from God's enemies. Are you aware of them? What are you doing about them?
- Guard your faith; set godly boundaries to protect your soul.
- Is living for God your passion?
- Are you currently aware of which boundaries you need to establish for yourself?
- Are you focusing your time and energy building your life? Or are you focused on the daily negativity around you?
- Only God can bring total fulfillment to your life. He's the one who designed you.

Prayer

Dearest Heavenly Father, there are areas in my life that I need to rebuild. Some attacks in my life are spiritual, mental, and emotional. To protect against this, I need godly boundaries. Some of the attacks I am aware of, but other attacks take me by surprise. Please help me to fortify my life for You. In Jesus' name, I pray. Amen!

ESTHER

Outline of the Book of Esther

1. Esther becomes queen—Esther 1:1–2:18
2. Haman plots to kill the Jews—Esther 2:19–3:15
3. Esther and Mordecai take action—Esther 4:1–5:14
4. Mordecai is honored; Haman is executed—Esther 6:1–7:10
5. The Jewish people are rescued and delivered—Esther 8:1–9:19
6. The Feast of Lots (Purim) is instituted—Esther 9:30–32
7. Mordecai and King Xerxes are revered—Esther 9:30–32

Have you ever let fear paralyze you from following through on trying something new? Why? Fear is real! It is also unavoidable. However, it was once shared with me, "Face your fears and they will disappear." I have lived facing my fear most of my life. I didn't want my fears to paralyze me. Facing your fears will have a positive impact on your life and the lives of others.

Fear could have paralyzed Esther and Mordecai. Esther and her cousin Mordecai were Jewish captives in the foreign land of Persia. By God's providence, Esther was selected queen by King Xerxes of Persia.

Haman was second in command to King Xerxes. Haman became enraged after Mordecai refused to bow down to him. Haman wanted Mordecai and all the Israelites killed, so he created a plot to trick King Xerxes into executing all the Jews in Persia. When Mordecai learned of the plot, he went to Esther and encouraged her to save their people. Esther risked her life entering the king's court without an invitation. Her actions saved all the Jewish people from being destroyed. Haman had gallows made so that King Xerxes would have Mordecai hung on the gallows. The hateful plan of Haman backfired, and Haman was hung on the same gallows that he had constructed.

God elevated Esther to the position of queen so she could help liberate her people. Because Mordecai was a God-fearing man, he was able to stand firm in his faith and to provide godly wisdom to his cousin Queen Esther.

My Verse for Golden Nuggets

> For if you keep silent at this time, relief and deliverance will rise for the Jews from another place, but you and your father's house will perish. And who knows whether you have not come to the kingdom for such a time as this? (Esther 4:14 ESV)

Practical Applications for Your Life Today

- Do you know that God created you for greatness?
- Your humility will allow God to exalt you.
- No matter how high you rise in life, never forget who blessed you to get there.
- By pursuing God's will with all your heart, you should be expecting God to use you.
- Remember, "you shall reap what you sow." Haman was executed on the very same gallows he made for someone else.
- God placed you in your position for a reason. Use it, don't abuse it.
- Seek God; speak up for yourself and others.

Prayer

Dearest Heavenly Father, I need You to assist me in becoming the powerful light that You created me to be. With so much darkness in the world, more people are needed that are living as lights for Jesus. Also, Father, help me to not allow wicked thoughts like Haman's to take root in my heart. In Jesus' name, I pray. Amen!

POETRY AND
WISDOM

JOB

Outline of the Book of Job

1. Job undergoes testing—Job 1:1–2:13
2. Job's three friends discuss his suffering—Job 3:1–31:40
3. Elihu contends that God punished Job to humble him—Job 32:1–37:24
4. God reveals His power and sovereignty to Job—Job 38:1–41:34
5. God scolds Job's friends and restores Job's family and fortune—Job 42:1–17

If you are like me, sometimes you wonder why certain things happen to you in your life. Someone once asked, "Who should it happen to instead of you?" In life, we want to enjoy the good times and always dodge the bad times. Unfortunately, it does not work that way. We tend to forget life is like a race with hurdles. If we are to win, we must make it over the obstacles.

God describes Job as His faithful servant, yet there were catastrophes Job had to overcome. Think of some of the worst things you have suffered in your life. Also, take some time to think about anyone else you may know who has experienced significant losses. With these thoughts in mind, let us read about Job.

The book of Job addresses how even good people experience suffering. Job was a righteous man who was wealthy. There came a time when he suffered sickness and lost everything, including his children. Yet in the midst of all this heartache and tragedy, he refused to blame God.

Job's friends tried to convince him that his suffering must be due to some unconfessed sin. Even Job's wife showed some disdain for God ("Curse God and die" in Job 2:9). Despite all the accusations, Job insisted on living with integrity. In the end, God spoke to Job and showed him His incredible power. God also rebuked Job's friends for their criticism. Job's wife and friends never understood that Job was engaged in an intense spiritual conflict. Job displayed incredible faith, even in the depths of his trials. As a result of his faith, God blessed Job immensely by giving him twice as much as he had before. Although Job was never told why he had to suffer so much, he understood that God was faithful and just.

My Verse for Golden Nuggets

Then the Lord said to Satan, "Have you considered my servant Job? There is no one on earth like him; he is blameless and upright, a man who fears God and shuns evil. And he still maintains his integrity, though you incited me against him to ruin him without any reason." (Job 2:3)

Practical Applications for Your Life Today

- Even when you are in trouble and hurting, be sure to maintain complete trust in God's love and power.
- Hard times can make your faith stronger. When hard times come knocking at your door, keep in mind that God wants to use this as an opportunity to strengthen you.
- Do not place your trust in yourself or others. Place all your faith and confidence in Jesus.
- There are times when you may feel that all hope is gone. Remember, you can never finish the race if you quit. Keep running toward Jesus.
- When you find yourself flat on your back, roll over onto your knees and pray.
- There are daily hurdles of various sizes you will need to overcome: some short and some tall. Always be ready to take a leap of faith with Jesus.

Prayer

Dear Heavenly Father, Job was a man full of integrity and faith. Even when he lost it all, he remained faithful. He did not permit his friends or his wife to influence him or convince him that he was in error. Father, I know that sometimes I allow my friends and other relationships to influence me in negative ways. As I spend more time meditating on Your word and trusting in Your guidance, You will see me through. I want to live boldly for You. In Jesus' name, I pray. Amen.

PSALMS

Outline of the Book of Psalms

1. Book 1: Psalms 1–41
2. Book 2: Psalms 42–72
3. Book 3: Psalms 73–89
4. Book 4: Psalms 90–106
5. Book 5: Psalms 107–150

The book of Psalms has some spiritual takeaways that will change your life forever. It has been a great source of comfort to God's people when facing heartache for centuries. The book of Psalms also teaches us what to do when we don't know the right words to use in talking to God. We can use songs and hymns to tell God about our problems and praise Him for His blessings. Let's look at the overview of the book of Psalms.

Psalms is a compilation of poems or songs, and it also served as a book of hymns for Israel. It contains expressions of praise, worship, thankfulness, and repentance. The lament psalms explore various feelings such as despair and suffering. Some psalms question why God permits evil. Other psalms celebrate God as the creator. There are also psalms expressing wonderment and delight for God. The book of Psalms contains 150 individual psalms by various authors such as David, Asaph, Solomon, and others. Many psalms do not have a recorded author. While the people first sang the psalms in ancient Israel, this book is for us as well. We can look to the psalms for comfort in times of despair, hope, fear, happiness, and joy. Each psalm is an expression of the heart. Depending on the depth of our problems, the psalms can be read at many different levels. The psalms remind us of God's unfailing and uncondi-tional love for humanity.

My Verses for Golden Nuggets

Trust in the LORD, and do good; so shalt thou dwell in the land, and ver-ily thou shalt be fed. Delight thyself also in the LORD; and he shall give thee the desires of thine heart. Commit thy way unto the LORD; trust also in him; and he shall bring it to pass. (Psalm 37:3–5) KJV

How can a young person stay on the path of purity? By living according to your word. I seek you with all my heart; do not let me stray from your commands. I have hidden your word in my heart that I might not sin against you. (Psalm 119:9–11)

Practical Applications for Your Life Today

- No matter what you are going through, good or bad, continue to praise God.
- Don't let trials and heartaches become distractions. Focusing on God during your trials will bring you peace.
- Do you ever feel down and depressed? Know that others have traveled down the same road and were able to find hope.
- You are fashioned and designed to show forth God's praises. Do you ever feel empty? Remember God is your comforter.
- The quality of your relationship with Jesus determines your quality of life.
- Where your prayers end, let your praises for God begin.
- Cultivate in your mind the habit of ceaseless praise. You cannot praise God and have fear paralyzing you at the same time. Praise more and worry less.

Prayer

Dear Heavenly Father, this book of Psalms is fantastic! It contains so many practical lessons for my daily life. If I am happy, sad, or depressed, I need to read Your Word. Please help me to remember that regardless of my circumstances, I need to look to You for everything. In Jesus' name, I pray. Amen.

PROVERBS

Outline of the Book of Proverbs

1. Benefits of wisdom and warnings against adultery and folly—Proverbs 1:1–9:18
2. Wise advice for all people—Proverbs 10:1–24:34
3. Wise advice for leaders—Proverbs 25:1–31:31

Are you wise? I would say, "Yes, you are!" Why? Because you are taking time from your busy schedule to learn more about the most essential book in the universe. Proverbs 1:7 sums it up: "The fear of the LORD is the beginning of knowledge, but fools despise wisdom and instruction." During the Christmas season, you will often see nativity scenes displayed. Part of the display shows the three wise men seeking and following the star to find Jesus. I once read this saying, "Wise men still seek Jesus." Who and what are you seeking?

We often pay a lot of money trying to acquire wisdom within the four walls of a school; however, this is merely human wisdom. Some attend seminars and study popular books in hopes of obtaining wisdom. As stated above, real wisdom comes from a fear of God. This particular fear is not the terror that God will bring harm to us. Instead, this fear is more along the lines of respect and deep admiration for God.

If you want to have godly wisdom, it is contained in God's Word. In fact, the book of Proverbs is like a book of ethics. By following this kind of wisdom, you will have a life enriched by God.

"If any of you lacks wisdom, let him ask God, who gives generously to all without reproach, and it will be given him" (James 1:5).

Proverbs is a collection of wise sayings that offer sound advice for your life. Most of the proverbs include wisdom on marriage, friendship, poverty, justice, love, family, wealth, warnings against laziness, drunkenness, and adultery. Acquiring godly wisdom takes focus, time, and discipline.

Most of Proverbs were written by Solomon, the wisest person that ever lived. Being wise does not guarantee you will not make sinful mistakes. Solomon fell prey to the lusts of the opposite sex. If you struggle with lust, you're not alone; continue to seek Jesus.

> For everything in the world-the lust of the flesh, the lust of the eyes, and the pride of life—comes not from the Father but from the world. The world and its desires pass away, but whoever does the will of God lives forever. (1 John 2:16–17)

Lust is unavoidable in this world. However, through God, Solomon offers some excellent advice in establishing godly boundaries in your life. God wants you to have His wisdom to protect and guide you.

My Verses for Golden Nuggets

The fear of the LORD is the beginning of knowledge, but fools despise wisdom and instruction. (Proverbs 1:7)

Trust in the LORD with all your heart and lean not on your own understanding; in all your ways submit to him, and he will make your paths straight. Do not be wise in your own eyes; fear the LORD and shun evil. (Proverbs 3:5–7)

Start children off on the way they should go, and even when they are old they will not turn from it. (Proverbs 22:6)

There is a way that appears to be right, but in the end it leads to death. (Proverbs 14:12)

Practical Applications for Your Life Today

- There are only two types of wisdom in the world. In this corner, you have earthly, unspiritual, and demonic wisdom. In the other corner, you have wisdom from heaven that is pure, peace-loving, and submissive (James 3:14–17).

- Wisdom brings calmness, kindness, and great contentment to your soul.
- Do you know that God generously gives out wisdom?
- What do you have in your life if God's wisdom is absent?
- What's the opposite of being wise?

Prayer

Dearest Heavenly Father, thank You for this beautiful book of wisdom. Thank You for reassuring me that there is great hope for me despite my struggles. Please increase my wisdom. In Jesus' name, I pray. Amen.

ECCLESIASTES

Outline of the Book of Ecclesiastes

1. The teacher relates his conclusions from his personal experiences during his search for meaning in life—Ecclesiastes 1:1–2:26
2. The teacher reflects on what he has learned about achievement, wealth, power, and other earthly pursuits—Ecclesiastes 3:1–5:20
3. The teacher gives practical advice on wisdom and obedience—Ecclesiastes 6:1–8:17
4. The teacher tells what he has concluded about destiny and God—Ecclesiastes 9:1–12:14

Many of us read books or watch videos on motivation or self-improvement. They are supposed to help us increase our quality of life. How long does all this additional advice and knowledge last?

What if I told you that there is a far more excellent motivational book than all the ones you have read in the past or ever will read? Sounds unbelievable, right? If you are still in doubt, simply read the book of Ecclesiastes. Here you will find out that money won't bring you happiness. If you have been busy gathering money, the teacher wants to burst your bubble; he says that's not what brings happiness. He knows from experience, for Solomon had more money and possessions than anyone who has ever lived.

The teacher also reiterates that all is vanity, meaning it brings emptiness from within. Your new clothing, your new car, your latest smartphone, and your new place to live, all these things are meaningless. Did the teacher mention those things that are not meaningless? Yes, he did. Let us look at the overview of this highly motivational book of Ecclesiastes.

Ecclesiastes is about the meaning of life. How do we make sense of events in life such as past sexual abuse, emotional and physical violence, rejection and neglect as a child, or being placed in a foster care system because of your parents? Maybe you were brought up in a home with parents who were addicted to drugs and alcohol? Perhaps none of the above categories pertain to you; however, there is always some form of dysfunction that has affected your life. Either way, these things can lead us to make poor choices. Ecclesiastes is narrated by the teacher, Solomon, David's son.

Solomon gives us the wisdom of understanding that all things have value. Ecclesiastes describes Solomon's search for the meaning of the supposed essential things in life, such as wisdom, pleasure, work, power, and riches. Ultimately, he concludes that all these things are meaningless. In the end, Solomon advises us that we should remember God, our Creator, and enjoy life, which is God's good gift to us. The conclusion is to give the utmost respect to God and to realize everything belongs to Him.

Ecclesiastes helps us set up the necessary boundaries to enjoy the life that we are given. Though life is to be enjoyed, there will also be things we do not understand. However, we find meaning and purpose in life when we honor God and follow his guidelines.

My Verses for Golden Nuggets

"Meaningless! Meaningless!" says the Teacher. "Utterly meaningless! Everything is meaningless. What do people gain from all their labors at which they toil under the sun?" (Ecclesiastes 1:2–3)

There is a time for everything, and a season for every activity under the heavens. (Ecclesiastes 3:1)

Whoever loves money never has enough; whoever loves wealth is never satisfied with their income. This, too is meaningless. (Ecclesiastes 5:10)

Let us hear the conclusion of the whole matter: Fear God, and keep his commandments: for this is the whole duty of man. (Ecclesiastes 12:13)

Practical Applications for Your Life Today

- Your life will always be a meaningless cycle when you do not follow God.

- When wisdom is obtained, direction comes, and life takes on a new meaning.
- Make wise use of your choices today. They are your destiny.
- Your hard work pays off when pleasing God is your engine of motivation.
- Are you acknowledging God in every area of your life?
- Develop a heart of thankfulness for every earthly and spiritual blessing.
- Live life in the present. Refuse to let the fears and worries of the past or future tarnish you today.
- Praise and thank God daily, work hard, and take time to enjoy God's blessings.
- At the end of your life, will you be able to say that you respected God and followed his guidance?

Prayer

Dear Heavenly Father, thank You so much for Your words. I need Your truth in my life daily. So many times I find myself chasing after the material things of this world because I want to be loved and appreciated by others. When others fall short, I allow their failure to bring me down. Then I question my self-worth. Help me please, Lord, to put all my heart and soul into You, Father, for You will never let me down. I need Your wisdom and strength. In Jesus' name, I pray. Amen.

SONG OF SONGS

Outline of the Book of Song of Songs

1. The bride thinks about Solomon in the palace—Song of Songs 1:1–3:5
2. The bride accepts the betrothal and looks forward to the joys of marriage—Song of Songs 3:6–5:1
3. The bride dreams of losing the groom, then finds him—Song of Songs 5:2–6:3
4. The bride and groom praise each other in passionate love—Song of Songs 6:4–8:14

Song of Songs (also sometimes known as the Song of Solomon) is a collection of poems between a lover and his beloved. It is the only book in the Bible that describes sexual relationships in somewhat explicit detail. Song of Songs offers a beautiful picture of love and marriage. God created sex to be enjoyed within the confines of marriage.

I thank God for His grace and forgiveness and His strength to overcome temptations. Song of Songs uses words full of passion and emotion to describe the lovers' emotional connection. It describes times of conflict, resolution, and a return to commitment. Some use this book to illustrate the relationship between Christ and His bride. However, the book primarily speaks of sexual love within the context of marriage. The bottom line is that it is a foundational message to take heed to true love's purity.

My Verses for Golden Nuggets

Scarcely had I passed them when I found the one my heart loves. I held him and would not let him go till I had brought him to my mother's house, to the room of the one who conceived me. (Song of Songs 3:4)

I am the rose of Sharon, and the lily of the valleys. As the lily among thorns, so is my love among the daughters. (Song of Songs 2:1–2)

He brought me to the banqueting house, and his banner over me was love. (Song of Songs 2:4)

Practical Applications for Your Life Today

- Sexual purity is only made possible by seeking God's guidance.
- A married relationship should be compared to the relationship of Christ and His church.

- Looking for true love? Look to God! Remember, "God is Love."
- God's love versus your fleshly lust. The choice is yours.
- Christ loves you unconditionally. So love others unconditionally.

Prayer

Dear Heavenly Father, thank You for this beautiful love story that depicts love in the purest form. I know lusting causes a shadow that taints my heart. I am incredibly grateful for the unconditional love. Help me, Father, not give up on myself because You will never give up on me. Please let Your love motivate me to live a pure life for You. In Jesus' name, I pray. Amen!

CLARIFICATION ON PROPHETS AND GENERATIONS

Here is an outline to help you comprehend the books written by the prophets. (There are many prophets in the Old Testament; however, God chose these select few to write history (His-story). Below you will find that these prophets spoke to different nations at different times. Some spoke to different generations, and some spoke to generations that overlapped other prophets. This can be really confusing because the prophets are basically relaying the same message—to turn back to God. So please keep this information in mind as you go through these books.

A breakdown of the prophets who wrote books, two of whom are listed in the Old Testament history section

The ministries of the prophets fell into three different periods, pre-captivity, captivity, and post-captivity. They were sent to Israel and Judah, except for Jonah, Obadiah, and Nahum, who were sent to Assyria and Edom. The northern kingdom went into captivity first, followed by the southern kingdom. At the beginning of the following books, I have listed to whom each book was written and their captivity status.

The seven books prophesied to/about *Judah* to warn them *before being taken into captivity*.

- Isaiah
- Jeremiah (before and during captivity)
- Lamentations (soon after the destruction of Jerusalem)
- Joel
- Micah
- Habakkuk
- Zephaniah

Two books prophesied to/about *Israel before being taken into captivity*.

- Hosea
- Amos

Two books prophesied to the Jewish people *during* the Babylonian captivity

- Ezekiel (before and during captivity)
- Daniel

Two books prophesied to/about another nation Assyria

- Jonah
- Nahum

One book prophesied to/about Edom (descendants of Esau)

- Obadiah

Five books to/about Judah *after the Babylonian captivity*

- Ezra *(priest)*
- Nehemiah *(not a prophet)*
- Haggai (the Israelites returned from Babylonian exile in different waves)
- Zechariah
- Malachi

Helpful Hints to Keep the Kingdoms and Enemies Straight

The letter I is next to J in the alphabet—two nations.
The letter A is next to B in the alphabet—two major enemies.
North and south—two geographical locations.
Israel is north. The *Assyrians* captured the *Israelites.*
Judah is south. The *Babylonians* captured *Judah.*

Near the end of the Old Testament, the new world power was the Persian Empire. After conquering the Assyrians and Babylonians, King Cyrus of Persia allowed the Jews to return to Jerusalem.

MAJOR

PROPHETS

ISAIAH

Judah: Before Captivity

Outline of the Book of Isaiah

1. Judgment—Isaiah 1:1–39:8
2. The transgressions of Judah and Israel—Isaiah 1:1–10:4
3. Judgment against the surrounding nations—Isaiah 10:5–23:18
4. The purpose of God's judgment—Isaiah 24:1–27:13
5. Jerusalem's true and false hope—Isaiah 28:1–35:10
6. Hezekiah's reign—Isaiah 36:1–39:8
7. Comfort—Isaiah 40:1–66:24
8. Israel's release from captivity—Isaiah 40:1–52:12
9. The future Messiah—Isaiah 52:13–59:21
10. The future kingdom—Isaiah 60:1–66:24

Have you ever been surprised by the outcome of an event? For example, the team you felt for sure was going to win ended up losing. Even during elections, we try to predict the outcome; however, in the end, something else happens.

Why? The reason is simple—man can only predict; however, God is the only one who truly knows the future.

Here's a saying that someone shared with me many years ago. "No one knows what the future holds; however, we know who holds the future." God knows the future, and He wants to give us guidance. That is why God used prophets to instruct, encourage, and warn people of impending doom if they do not change their ways.

Isaiah means "salvation is of the Lord." This book starts with a message of impending judgment. At this particular time, the Assyrians had already destroyed the northern kingdom, and they are now getting ready to capture the southern kingdom, Judah. Isaiah relayed God's message to Judah that if the people were willing to change their hearts and turn back to God, He would restore them, and judgment would be averted.

Instead of seeking what was right, they came up with their own plans to try to save themselves. Judah tried to make an agreement with God's enemies, Assyria and Egypt. How foolish. Sin will distort your thinking to the point where you will think that you are smarter than God. Eventually, Judah was captured by the Babylonians.

Toward the end of Isaiah, there is a message of hope. God promised that He would deliver His people out of Babylon. Out of the many prophets, Isaiah drives home that salvation and deliverance would come through Jesus. However, this would not be understood until the time of Jesus. Jesus was the Savior to come out of Judah (the tribe of Judah) to bring universal redemption for both Jews and Gentiles. What an honor it is to be a part of God's plan of reconciliation and redemption.

My Verses for Golden Nuggets

Therefore the Lord himself shall give you a sign; Behold, a virgin shall conceive, and bear a son, and shall call his name Immanuel. (Isaiah 7:14) KJV

But he was pierced for our transgressions, he was crushed for our iniquities; the punishment that brought us peace was on him, and by his wounds we are healed. We all, like sheep, have gone astray, each of us has turned to our own way; and the LORD has laid on him the iniquity of us all. He was oppressed and afflicted, yet he did not open his mouth; he was led like a lamb to the slaughter, and as a sheep before its shearers is silent, so he did not open his mouth. By oppression and judgment, he was taken away. Yet who of his generation protested? For he was cut off from the land of the living; for the transgression of my people he was punished. He was assigned a grave with the wicked, and with the rich in his death, though he had done no violence, nor was any deceit in his mouth. (Isaiah 53:5–9) KJV

"No weapon formed against you shall prosper, and every tongue *which* rises

against you in judgment You shall condemn. This *is* the heritage of the servants
of the Lord, and their righteousness *is*
from Me," Says the LORD. (Isaiah 54:17
NKJV)

Practical Applications for Your Life Today

- Isn't it comforting to know that God has established a plan for Jesus to come and to save you
  from your sins?
- Anyone not living for God becomes His enemy.
  What you do daily determines who you are living
  for.
- God has zero respect for an idol. God will destroy
  every idol and every idol worshipper.
- An idol is anything in your life that takes the place
  of God.
- God's instructions always produce godly results.
- Strive to allow God into every choice you make,
  big or small.

Prayer

Dearest Heavenly Father, I know that You hold my
future in Your hands. You know my struggles. You know
the things that take me captive. I need Your strength, forgiveness, and direction so that I can be the godly person
You created me to be. In Jesus' name, I pray. Amen.

JEREMIAH

Judah: Before and during Captivity

Outline of the Book of Jeremiah

1. God's call of Jeremiah—Jeremiah 1:1–19
2. Warnings to Judah—Jeremiah 2:1–35:19
3. Jeremiah's persecution and suffering—Jeremiah 36:1–38:28
4. Fall of Jerusalem and consequences—Jeremiah 39:1–45:5
5. Prophecies about the nations—Jeremiah 46:1–51:64
6. Historical appendix—Jeremiah 52:1–34

During this time, the Lord tells Jeremiah, "Backsliding Israel has shown herself more righteous than treacherous Judah" (Jeremiah 3:11). God is saying that Judah has stooped to a new level of evil. God used the wicked, ungodly King Nebuchadnezzar of Babylon to punish His people for their disobedience, disregard, and lack of respect for God's commands.

Jeremiah started as a prophet at a young age. He labored for over forty years proclaiming a message of doom to a stubborn people. He was very humble and wanted to do all he could to please the Lord. Jeremiah had it rough, really rough. He was hated and persecuted by his own countrymen. He was a wanted man for a good portion of his ministry. The political and religious leaders in Judah hated him. Because of God's message, he ended up being confined in a dungeon, beaten, and almost killed. Jeremiah witnessed the destruction and plunder of Jerusalem. The leaders are killed and the captives are taken to Babylon. Where was God when all of this was going on? God was right there protecting him. Yes! You will be challenged because of your faith. However, challenges will come regardless of whether or not you live for God.

> Blessed are those who are persecuted because of righteousness, for theirs is the kingdom of heaven. Blessed are you when people insult you, persecute you and falsely say all kinds of evil against you because of me. Rejoice and be glad, because great is your reward in heaven, for in the same way, they persecuted the prophets who were before you. (Matthew 5:10–12 NKJV)

Through all of this, Jeremiah kept on standing, speaking, and warning people about God.

Jeremiah is also known as the weeping prophet. Just because he cried, this didn't make him weak, far from it. As you have read above, Jeremiah was bold and on fire for the

Lord. Jeremiah did not weep for himself; he wept for God's people because of the pain and loss they suffered. He wept over and over again because the people repeatedly sinned yet never repented. Despite all of this, Jeremiah never lost his faith in God.

My Verses for Golden Nuggets

Before I formed you in the womb I knew you, before you were born I set you apart; I appointed you as a prophet to the nations. (Jeremiah 1:5)

But if I say, "I will not mention his word or speak anymore in his name," his word is in my heart like a fire, a fire shut up in my bones. I am weary of holding it in; indeed, I cannot. (Jeremiah 20:9)

"For I know the plans I have for you," declares the Lord, "plans to prosper you and not to harm you, plans to give you hope and a future." (Jeremiah 29:11)

Call to me and I will answer you and tell you great and unsearchable things you do not know. (Jeremiah 33:3)

Practical Applications for Your Life Today

- Are you aware that God formed your every detail in your mother's womb?
- Even when the odds are stacked against you, you must stick with God's plan.
- Having boldness in God brings joy, pain, honor, and glory to God.
- If you are not giving your best to God, you have not found your purpose for living.
- Are you living your life courageously or recklessly?
- Is your view of success based on God's perspective or the world's? He that dies with the most material possessions still dies.
- There are no good excuses for not living for God.
- Rejection and rejoicing are a part of living for Jesus. "They departed from the presence of the council, rejoicing that they were counted worthy to suffer shame for his name" (Acts 5:41 KJV).
- Do you want to live free and victorious?

Prayer

Dearest Heavenly Father, thank You for Your love and guidance. Thank You for having an excellent plan for my life. Help me not to follow after my fleshly desires as the plan for my life. Often I stumble over myself and get tripped up by the fear of what others may say or think about me. Only You can help me stay rooted and grounded in Your excellent plans for my life. In Jesus' name, I pray. Amen.

LAMENTATIONS

During or Soon After the Destruction of Jerusalem

Outline of the Book of Lamentations

1. Jeremiah grieves over Jerusalem's suffering—Lamentations 1:1–22
2. Sin brings the wrath of God—Lamentations 2:1–22
3. God never abandons His own—Lamentations 3:1–66
4. Jerusalem's glory has been lost—Lamentations 4:1–22
5. Jeremiah asks God to restore His people—Lamentations 5:1–22

Lamentations is the passionate expression of grief, sorrow, and weeping.

Why should I be reading Lamentations when God clearly says we should "rejoice in the Lord always"? Because the same God says, "There is a time for everything, for everything under heaven."

There are times of joy, laughter, and even times of crying. Yes, there are times when you need to cry unto the

Lord. Jeremiah saw the many things that were happening in his time and in the future of God's people. Jeremiah began to weep for the Israelites. Seeing Jerusalem destroyed and God's people taken into captivity broke his heart. However, just as you read in his previous book, Jeremiah reminds the Israelites that God is faithful and merciful. His arms are open wide to those who will turn and seek Him. God wants to embrace and comfort His people. However, they must want to live for Him. This collection of laments should remind us of the evil, injustices, and brokenness that continues in this fallen world when people reject God. These are things we should all be weeping about regularly.

My Verses for Golden Nuggets

Is it nothing to you, all you who pass by? Look around and see. Is any suffering like my suffering that was inflicted on me, that the LORD brought on me in the day of his fierce anger? (Lamentations 1:12)

My eyes fail from weeping, I am in torment within; my heart is poured out on the ground because my people are destroyed, because children and infants faint in the streets of the city. (Lamentations 2:11)

The steadfast love of the LORD never ceases; his mercies never come to an end; they are new every morning; great is your faithfulness. (Lamentations 3:22)

Restore us to yourself, O Lord, that we may return; renew our days as of old. (Lamentations 5:21)

Practical Applications for Your Life Today

- God's love, compassion, and mercy are always there for you. His love never fails.
- You should never expect God to reward ungodly behaviors. He is always willing and longing to forgive you when you honestly turn to live for Him.
- Are you sharing God's compassion with others?
- When was the last time you honestly cried or poured out your heart to God for something that broke your heart?
- Rejoicing in the misfortunes of others will only bring misfortunes to you. "Do not gloat when your enemy falls; when they stumble, do not let your heart rejoice, or the LORD will see and disapprove and turn his wrath away from them" (Proverbs 24:17–18).
- Imagine how a parent feels when they see their child confused and hurting. Remember, you are God's child; He knows how to comfort you.

Prayer

Dearest Heavenly Father, I am Your child. You are the one who created me and know everything about me. It must be sad for You to see Your children struggling on their own when You are right there willing and longing to help and heal them. Please, Father, help me as Your child. You are the only one who hears my cries, knows my struggles, and can strengthen me. In Jesus' name, I pray. Amen.

EZEKIEL

Judah: Before and during Captivity

Outline of the Book of Ezekiel

1. Prophecies about destruction—Ezekiel 1:1–24:27
2. Ezekiel's appointment by God—Ezekiel 1:1–3:27
3. Revelations of sin and God's judgment—Ezekiel 4:1–22:31
4. God's punishment is inescapable—Ezekiel 23:1–24:27
5. Prophecies condemning foreign nations—Ezekiel 25:1–32:32
6. Oracles against Ammon, Moab, Edom, Philistia, Tyre, Sidon, Egypt—Ezekiel 25:1–30:26
7. Oracles against foreign countries' rulers—Ezekiel 31:1–32:32
8. Prophesies of hope and restoration of Israel—Ezekiel 33:1–48:35
9. Shepherds who will protect and restore Israel—Ezekiel 33:1–36:38
10. Raising dry bones; restoring hope—Ezekiel 37:1–39:29

11. The new temple filled with God's glory—Ezekiel 40:1–47:23
12. Dividing the land among the tribes—Ezekiel 48:1–48:35

Every day negative news penetrates our ears, minds, and spirits. Have you ever heard of the coronavirus? It has dominated and affected our world, yet the coronavirus is nothing compared to what will happen to this world when Jesus returns.

Let God be your protector. While man's protection can only go so far, God's everlasting protection is what you need. Anywhere you turn, there is devastation because we live in a fallen world. The vast majority of the world does not care about living for God and is not concerned about the end of time. God has been gracious enough to write things down in the Bible for you to read and learn. Have you ever realized something only after it was too late? How did you feel? Well, the good thing is you are still alive to see another day. However, there will be a time when things are final and irreversible, just like during Ezekiel's lifetime.

Ezekiel's name means "God is strong." He was a prophet called by God. His message is to the captives from Judah, those who were already in Babylon. God's people in exile were struggling with disbelief and discouragement. They are probably wondering what happened. "Why didn't we listen?" Some were probably saying, "It's not my fault." Just as those in Jerusalem (Judah) who could not believe that God would allow the city and the temple to be destroyed, now Israel is facing the same fate. Ezekiel foretold the events that were going to happen to Jerusalem. Its destruction was inevitable. God wanted to show His children that their sins had severe consequences. Eventually, the children of Israel confessed their sins and turned back to God for help. God gave Ezekiel a vision of a valley of dry bones coming to life, which represented God's promise to restore Jerusalem and His children.

My Verses for Golden Nuggets

> So I got up and went out to the plain. And the glory of the LORD was standing there, like the glory I had seen by the Kebar River, and I fell facedown. (Ezekiel 3:23)

> Therefore say to the people of Israel, "This is what the Sovereign Lord says: Repent! Turn from your idols and renounce all your detestable practices!" (Ezekiel 14:6)

> So I spoke to the people in the morning, and in the evening my wife died. The next morning I did as I had been commanded. (Ezekiel 24:18)

> I will give you a new heart and put a new spirit in you; I will remove from you

your heart of stone and give you a heart of flesh. (Ezekiel 36:26)

He asked me, "Son of man, can these bones live?" I said, "Sovereign LORD, you alone know." Then he said to me, "Prophesy to these bones and say to them, 'Dry bones, hear the word of the LORD!' This is what the Sovereign LORD says to these bones: I will make breath enter you, and you will come to life. I will attach tendons to you and make flesh come upon you and cover you with skin; I will put breath in you, and you will come to life. Then you will know that I am the LORD." (Ezekiel 37:3–6)

Practical Applications for Your Life Today

- Which one of God's warnings are you trying to avoid?
- God is always willing to go above and beyond to get your attention and move you to live righteously.
- God specializes in bringing dead things to life.
- God had Ezekiel speak to a valley of dry bones to bring forth life. Are there dry bones in your life?
- Are you allowing God to strengthen and guide you in your daily life?
- Are you willing to let God control every detail of your life?

- Are you creating a prison of negativity, or are you creating a life with a landslide full of blessings?
- Victories in your life are inevitable when you walk with God.

Prayer

Dearest Heavenly Father, thank You for giving me another opportunity today to draw closer to You. Help me identify those things preventing me from getting closer to You. Even though they may be a secret to others, I know that my thoughts are no secret to You. Here are some of my thoughts that I need to turn over to You and some actions I need to turn away from. Thank You. In Jesus' name, I pray. Amen.

DANIEL

Judah: During Captivity

Outline of the Book of Daniel

1. Introduction and Daniel's interpretation of Nebuchadnezzar's great statue dream—Daniel 1:1–2:49
2. Shadrach, Meshach, and Abednego rescued from the fiery furnace—Daniel 3:1–30
3. Nebuchadnezzar's dream and subsequent humiliation followed by his restoration after humbling himself—Daniel 4:1–37
4. The moving finger writes an ominous warning, and Daniel prophesied destruction—Daniel 5:1–31
5. God saves Daniel in the lion's den—Daniel 6:1–28
6. Daniel's vision of four beasts—Daniel 7:1–28
7. Daniel's vision of a ram, goat, and small horn—Daniel 8:1–27
8. Daniel's prayer answered with the revelation of the seventy years—Daniel 9:1–27
9. Daniel's vision of the final great war—Daniel 10:1–12:13

The book of Daniel is one of the most exciting books in the Bible. Some events that happened in Daniel's time are happening today. Okay, no one is threatening to throw you into a lion's den; however, in God's word, we are warned about a lion that prowls around seeking to destroy our souls.

"Be alert and of sober mind. Your enemy, the devil, prowls around like a roaring lion looking for someone to devour" (1 Peter 5:8).

If the devil can distract us, he can destroy us. Take a close look at how you spend your time, and it will provide a clear indication of whether you are in the lion's den being consumed by the enemy. You must be aware of those things that are wasting your time and threatening your faith. For instance, being a prisoner to technology, believing the abnormal is normal or assuming ungodly behavior is acceptable to God are some examples of ways that we can be deceived.

I believe the saying "time flies" is a true statement. At the end of your life, what would you wish for? More time to watch sports, play video games, follow human idols on social media, and spend more time with ungodly people? Or maybe you will be thankful for the way that you lived your life for Jesus. We should strive to live life in a way that pleases Jesus. Let's look at Daniel to see if he can provide us with some wonderful examples of how to live for God.

Daniel and his friends are so inspirational. They took a stand for God even when everyone around them bowed down to man-made idols. We can learn lessons from Daniel and his friends on how to be steadfast even in the face of today's modern idols.

Daniel was a prophet who was among the first group of people carried off to be exiled in Babylon. Daniel and his amazing friends encouraged one another by their faithfulness and devotion to honor God. After being taken into captivity, they were able to excel and serve the Babylonian King Nebuchadnezzar.

Daniel and his friends remained faithful, even while in a hostile environment. As a result of their devotion to God, Daniel and his friends were given prominent positions in the Babylonian Empire. When you choose to live for God, you will receive God's favor in your life. Daniel and his friends trusted God even when they faced death for practicing their faith. God protected Daniel and his friends because of their devotion and loyalty to God.

Not only did God take care of them, but he also took care of their enemies. So when people are against you, don't retaliate. Instead, get on your knees and fight like a man or woman of God. Daniel and his friends were "prayer warriors."

After Babylon fell to Persia, Daniel continued serving in King Darius' court. Daniel was given prophecies and visions that enabled him to foresee the suffering his people would endure as well as the future restoration of Israel. He also prophesied the first and second coming of Christ. Daniel's visions reveal the power of God over everything, past, present, and future.

My Verses for Golden Nuggets

"Look!" he answered, "I see four men loose, walking in the midst of the fire; and they are not hurt, and the form of the fourth is like the Son of God." (Daniel 3:25) NKJV

The king was overjoyed and gave orders to lift Daniel out of the den. When Daniel was raised from the den, no wound was found on him, because he had trusted in his God. The king commanded that the men who had falsely accused Daniel be brought out. The king had the men, their wives, and children thrown into the lions' den. Before they reached the floor of the den, the lions overpowered them and crushed all their bones. Then King Darius wrote to all the nations and peoples of every language in all the earth: "May you prosper greatly! "I issue a decree that in every part of my kingdom, people must fear and reverence Daniel's God. "For he is the living God and he endures forever; his kingdom will not be destroyed, his dominion will never end. He rescues, and he saves; he performs signs and wonders in the heavens and on the earth. He has rescued Daniel from the power of the lions." (Daniel 6:23–27)

Practical Applications for Your Life Today

- How you spend your time and who you spend time with can be a good indicator of your destiny.
- Do you want to know your purpose in life? Give God your best, and He will do the rest.
- You can always make excuses, but they are empty and a waste of time. It is better to admit your shortcomings and seek God's help.
- You must be direct about living your life for God.
- Stay focused and avoid being tricked into conforming to the world around you.
- Strive to maintain your integrity at all times. Even when you mess up, have the integrity to fess up to your mistakes.

Prayer

Dearest Heavenly Father, thank You for your protection and for allowing me to be alive today. At any given time, my life could have been cut short. Help me to trust You in every situation. Father, I also want to ask You to forgive me and to provide me with boldness to be a light in this world. In Jesus' name, I pray. Amen.

MINOR

PROPHETS

HOSEA

Israel: Before Captivity

Outline of the Book of Hosea

1. Hosea's faithless wife and her children—Hosea 1:1–11
2. God punishes and restores Israel—Hosea 2:1–23
3. Hosea redeems his wife just as God will redeem Israel—Hosea 3:1–5
4. Hosea levels God's charges against Israel—Hosea 4:1–8:14
5. Israel's punishment for being unfaithful described—Hosea 9:1–10:15
6. God loves and restores Israel—Hosea 11:1–14:9

Would you knowingly date or marry a prostitute? What would you think if you knew someone who married a prostitute? What would you say if, after they married and had children, she returned to her former lifestyle? Well, this is precisely what the prophet Hosea did. He married "a lady of the evening."

In the New Testament, Jesus told some religious people this, "Truly I tell you, the tax collectors and the prostitutes are entering the kingdom of God ahead of you" (Matthew 21:31). In the genealogy of Jesus, a former prostitute named Rahab is in Jesus' direct bloodline. You can read about this in Matthew 1:5 and Joshua 2:1. These are beautiful examples of God's unconditional love for you and me. Anyway, back to Hosea.

Hosea was a prophet who came from the northern kingdom of Israel. This book talks about Hosea's love for his wife, Gomer, even though she was unfaithful. After they had children, Gomer returned to prostituting herself again and ended up becoming a slave.

God commanded Hosea to buy Gomer back and restore her to their family. God used this demonstration of love as a symbol of His unconditional love for His people. Even though God loved the Israelites, He still allowed them to suffer the consequences of their sin. They would eventually repent and turn back to God and be restored once more.

My Verses for Golden Nuggets

What can I do with you, Ephraim? What can I do with you, Judah? Your love is like the morning mist, like the early dew that disappears. Therefore, I cut you in pieces with my prophets, I killed you with the words of my mouth—then my judgments go forth like the sun. For I desire mercy, not sacrifice, and acknowledg-

ment of God rather than burnt offerings.
(Hosea 6:4–6)

I will heal their waywardness and love
them freely, for my anger has turned away
from them. (Hosea 14:4)

Practical Applications for Your Life Today

- Are you thankful that God's love is unconditional?
- Is your love for your spouse and others unconditional?
- Do you ever get your idea of love confused with God's love?
- Have you ever compared your sins to other people's sins? Judging?
- God will provide you with the strength to resist temptation in this world.
- Are you embracing God's unconditional love daily?

Prayer

Dearest Heavenly Father, this is a compelling and moving true story revealing Your demonstration of unconditional love. Help me truly understand Your grace and forgiveness when I fall into sin. Then, Father, help me embrace Your unconditional strength to live righteously for You. In Jesus' name, I pray. Amen.

JOEL

Judah: Before Captivity

Outline of the Book of Joel

1. Locusts invade Israel, signaling the coming Day of the Lord—Joel 1:1–20
2. A foreign army thunders in to deliver God's punishment—Joel 2:1–17
3. Our ever-merciful God restores Israel—2:18–32
4. God judges the nations, then dwells among His people—3:1–21

Have you ever walked down the street only to run into a swarm of gnats flying around you? Have you ever had bees or flies buzzing around you? How about being surrounded by so many insects that you couldn't see anything except darkness and destruction? Let's see what a man of God and an abundance of locusts is all about.

Joel's name means "the Lord is God." God allowed a devastating swarm of locusts to invade Judah because they turned their backs on God. This event was catastrophic because of Israel's agricultural economy. Joel called the people to repentance. Then he warned that this natural disaster is nothing compared to the coming "great and very terrible" day of the Lord (2:11). Joel tells them they will be invaded by a dreadful army that will make the locust invasion seem mild by comparison. Joel appeals to the people to repent and turn back to God.

My Verses for Golden Nuggets

> Rend your heart and not your garments. Return to the LORD your God, for he is gracious and compassionate, slow to anger and abounding in love, and he relents from sending calamity. (Joel 2:13)

> The Lord will roar from Zion and thunder from Jerusalem; the earth and the heavens will tremble. But the Lord will be a refuge for his people, a stronghold for the people of Israel. (Joel 3:16)

Practical Applications for Your Life Today

- God has issued you many warnings of coming judgment. Will you heed them or ignore them?
- How unfair would it be if God did not give you guidance on how to avoid His coming judgment? Thank God for His instructions in the Bible.
- No matter the hardships you will go through in life, the worst is yet to come without Jesus.

- Are you grateful that God allowed you to live another day?
- Humility and godly sorrow are necessary to restore your relationship with God.

Prayer

Dearest Heavenly Father, I am so thankful that You have given me another day. I can see that You do keep Your word without exception. Throughout the beginning of time, You have always guided Your people. Be with me, Lord, as I travel down the path that leads to You. In Jesus' name, I pray. Amen.

AMOS

Israel: Before Captivity

Outline of the Book of Amos

1. God condemns the surrounding nations, Judah, and Israel—Amos 1:1–2:16
2. God judges Israel's sins—Amos 3:1–5:17
3. Amos prophesies exile—Amos 5:18–6:14
4. Amos reports his visions of God's wrath—Amos 7:1–9:10
5. God promises to restore Israel—Amos 9:11–15

Today, many of us may enjoy the numerous benefits of the modern world. You may have a nice place to live. You may also have smartphones, iPads, internet, and so much more. There may be convenience stores and restaurants all around you. Regardless of where you live or the material possessions you have, you may be feeling like you are "successful."

Someone once shared this quote with me, "Success is found in Jesus, and failure is found anywhere outside of Jesus." God is not impressed with your material possessions. Many people confuse material blessings with spiritual blessings. God is crystal clear that your soul is the most valuable thing you possess. If you lose your soul, you have lost everything. "What good does it do for someone to gain the whole world, yet lose their soul? What can anyone give in exchange for their soul?" (Matthew 16:26).

The events happening today in our modern world are similar to what was occurring during Amos' time. The people of Israel in the north enjoyed many luxuries because of God's blessings. Amos' warning applies to us today. We do not want to get complacent or comfortable with our material blessings.

The name Amos means "burden or burden bearer." He carried the heavy message from God to the rebellious and stubborn Israelites. During this time, Israel was blessed with fortune and great riches. Their prosperity led to their spiritual decline. Because of their so-called success, the Israelites felt they could live without God.

Unfortunately, they had forgotten that everything they enjoyed came from God. Amos confronted them about their lack of respect toward God. Through Amos' visions, he warned the people of the great judgment that was coming because they were being unfaithful to God. They were mistreating the poor, being sexually immoral, and even committing murder.

God told Amos that He would use a plumb line to measure how well the Israelites were doing. A plumb line is a string with a weight attached to the bottom end. A person holds the other end from near the top of a wall, allowing gravity to pull the weight down, making the string perfectly vertical. This perfectly straight line is lined up next to a wall to verify the structure is inline. If the building aligns with the plumb line, the chances are that the structure will be strong and sturdy because the walls are straight.

If the building walls are out of alignment, the structure is unsound, and there is a strong chance it will eventually collapse. In Matthew 7:24–25, Jesus told a story about two men who each built a house. One of the men was wise and built his house on a rock foundation. By contrast, the foolish man chose to build his house on the sand. When violent storms came, which one of the homes remained? Of course, the one that survived was built on the rock foundation, which represents Jesus. The sand foundation represents a foundation based on man's works, ensuring it is guaranteed to collapse when life's trials come.

Because the Israelites failed to repent, the storms that God promised came upon them. Amos told them, "Prepare to meet your God" (Amos 4:12). As always, God's predictions came to pass just as promised. The Israelites experienced death and destruction, and the survivors were taken captive by the Babylonians.

Amos also foretold of the future hope promised to those who sought to honor God. He explained that God would offer total restoration for those who had a change of heart and change of behavior.

My Verses for Golden Nuggets

Do two walk together unless they
have agreed to do so? (Amos 3:3)

And the Lord asked me, "What do you see, Amos?" "A plumb line," I replied. Then the Lord said, "Look, I am setting a plumb line among my people Israel; I will spare them no longer." (Amos 7:8)

This is what the LORD says to Israel: "Seek me and live." (Amos 5:4)

In that day I will restore David's fallen shelter—I will repair its broken places and restore its ruins—and will rebuild it as it used to be, so that they may possess the remnant of Edom and all the nations that bear my name, declares the Lord, who will do these things. (Amos 9:11–12)

Practical Applications for Your Life Today

- Have you become too comfortable with your material blessings?
- Complacency often happens with little to no notice.
- Use God's Word as your plumb line to continually measure your Christian walk.
- Always remember that God notices everything you do, whether good or bad.
- Treat others in a way that would be pleasing to God.

- God genuinely cares about the poor and less fortunate, so should you.
- Living a godly lifestyle is the richest way to live.
- Feeling prideful or self-sufficient is detrimental to your spiritual health.
- Being in denial can cause you to live an unfulfilled life.

Prayer

Dear Heavenly Father, please help me use only Your Word as the measuring instrument for my life. I understand that being wise means building my life on the stable, unmovable, and unchanging foundation of Jesus. I need Jesus! It's in His name I pray. Amen.

OBADIAH

Edom: Before Judah's Captivity

Outline of the Book of Obadiah

1. Seeing God's principle of justice—Obadiah 1–9
2. Viewing God's actions against injustice—Obadiah 10–14
3. God promises to restore and protect Israel—Obadiah 15–21

Have you ever let pride get in the way of your relationship with your spouse? What about your children, your parents, your employer, or your neighbor? Do you often argue and feel you have to always justify your position because of pride?

Jesus shares a parable about two sons. The father told his first son to go work in the vineyard. He told his father *"no"* but then later changed his mind and went. The second son was also told to go and work in the vineyard. Unlike the first son, he immediately said *"yes"* but chose not to go. Jesus asked, "Which one of the sons did what their father asked them to do?" Of course, the answer is the first son.

I thought of this parable because although the first son said "no," he had a change of heart and went. He was given a chance to make a correction. This was not the case for the Edomites. They were out of chances. Despite being descendants of Abraham, God gave them a death sentence and promised that they would be destroyed forever. God is the judge, jury, and executioner, and there is no court of appeals for His rulings. Let us read Obadiah and, hopefully, we can learn from their mistakes.

God had enough with the Edomites. This was not the first time they refused to help their relatives in times of need. "Pride comes before a fall" (Proverbs 16:18), meaning when you're riding proudly on your high horse, be assured you will eventually hit the ground face-first. "Facedown" is an excellent position for the prideful person because it's the perfect posture for prayer.

Let's look at the geographical location of the Edomites. Because of their prime location, they felt that they were untouchable. Their arrogance was because they were on top of Mount Seir. How foolish for anyone to believe they are untouchable or unreachable by God? Being prideful can cause you to think foolishly.

The name Obadiah means "servant of the Lord" or "worshipper of Yahweh." Obadiah is the shortest book in the Bible, having only twenty-one verses. The Edomites (from Edom) and Israelites (from Judah) were closely related. Esau and Jacob were twin brothers. Esau's descendants were known as the Edomites, and Jacob's descendants were the Israelites.

Obadiah's prophecy condemned how the Edomites treated the Israelites. Through Obadiah's visions, the Lord announced that Edom's kingdom would be destroyed because of their arrogance and sins. When Judah needed help from the Edomites, they refused to lift a finger to help their brothers. If that wasn't bad enough, they rejoiced over the Babylonian army, plundering them. The Edomites even captured some of the Israelites trying to escape and turned them over to the Babylonians. This betrayal was the final straw. God promised that Edom would receive the consequences of their actions. The book may be short, but it is very powerful. In this book, Edom's fate was sealed. There was no possibility of deliverance offered. Let's see what other lessons we can learn from Obadiah.

My Verses for Golden Nuggets

The pride of your heart has deceived you, you who live in the clefts of the rocks and make your home on the heights, you who say to yourself, "Who can bring me down to the ground?" "Though you soar like the eagle and make your nest among the stars, from there I will bring you down," declares the LORD. Because of the violence against your brother Jacob, you will be covered with shame; you will be destroyed forever. Deliverers will go up on Mount Zion to govern the mountains of Esau. And the kingdom will be the Lord's. (Obadiah 3, 4, 10, 21)

Practical Applications for Your Life Today

- You are never out of reach from the hand of God.
- Do you want to be judged guilty by God?
- If you have pride, surrender it or get ready for your downfall.
- Pride harms you and your relationships.
- When others attack you, hold on to the promises of God.
- Your only place of refuge is in the presence of God.
- God helps you, and He expects you to help others.
- God will always give you the ability to accomplish His will.

Prayer

Dearest Heavenly Father, there are prideful things that I need to surrender and lay on Your altar. I know that pride is not healthy for me, spiritually, physically, or emotionally. Please provide me with the grace, strength, and humility to work daily to better do your will. In Jesus' name, I pray. Amen!

JONAH

To Nineveh, Capital City of Assyria: Before Israel's Captivity

Outline of the Book of Jonah

1. Jonah rejects God's call and heads to the docks to find a ship—Jonah 1:1–14
2. To calm the storm, the crew hesitantly threw Jonah into the sea where God provides a great fish to save him—Jonah 1:15–16
3. After being in the belly of the fish for three days, Jonah cries out to God, repents, and is now willing to carry out God's mission. The fish vomits Jonah onto dry land—Jonah 1:17–2:10
4. Jonah preaches in Nineveh, and the people repented, causing God to spare them—Jonah 3:1–10
5. Angry at God's compassion, Jonah complains when a vine that God made for Jonah for his shade dies. God rebukes Jonah for being more concerned with a vine than the 120,000 souls in Nineveh—Jonah 4:1–11

Picture this scenario: Your friend tells you that he just spent three days underwater in the belly of a fish. After three days and three nights, the large fish spit him out on the shore. Then he says that God instructed him to go on a three-day journey to a certain city. Would you believe him?

You would probably think that he or she was out of their mind. Well, this event actually happened to a man named Jonah. With God, all things are possible. Jonah learned that he could not escape from God and that God is in control of everything. Can you run away from God without facing severe consequences? What are some of the other lessons to be learned from the book of Jonah?

Jonah was a prophet called by God to preach in the wicked city of Nineveh. (Nineveh is located in today's Iraq.) Nineveh was the capital city of Assyria. God sent Jonah to warn the people of Nineveh of His impending judgment. Assyria was a nation known for its wickedness and brutality. Jonah did not want to see God spare them, so he tried to run away. Jonah went in a different direction by boarding a ship going west toward Tarshish. While on that ship, a great storm arose that threatened to destroy the ship. The sailors were scared to death as they fought to save the ship. Meanwhile, Jonah was sleeping below deck.

Wow! How could Jonah sleep while a horrible storm was going on and while being disobedient to God? The truth is that Jonah had a bad case of denial. What is your level of denial? Are you able to sleep at night while being defiant and disobedient to God?

Jonah thought he could escape from God, but God knew exactly where Jonah was. Here's an even more powerful thought: God already knew that Jonah would try to run away from Him.

There were negative consequences for Jonah's actions. His denial and disobedience also affected the people around him. The same is true for you. You may feel that your actions against God only affect you, and you're not hurting anybody. Not true! Your actions or lack of actions affect others, especially those closest to you. Some of those who might be affected are parents, children, grandchildren, siblings, unborn children, and even your future spouse, and the list goes on.

The sailors decided that this storm came because of someone on board. They cast lots, and the lot fell on Jonah. Reluctantly, they threw him overboard after he told them it would be all right. God caused a large fish to swallow him. Jonah was in the fish's belly for three days and three nights. While inside the fish, Jonah had a change of attitude and began praying a beautiful prayer to God.

When God saw fit, He ordered the fish to vomit Jonah out on dry land. Jonah begrudgingly went to the people of Nineveh and told them of God's impending doom if they refused to follow God. The people of Nineveh listened to Jonah. They immediately started changing their ways and cried out to God for forgiveness. In response to their change of heart, God responded with love, mercy, and forgiveness. Jonah was used by God to spread the news that God desires people of all nations to follow Him.

My Verses for Golden Nuggets

> So they asked him, "Tell us, who is responsible for making all this trouble for us? What kind of work do you do? Where do you come from? What is your country? From what people are you?" He answered, "I am a Hebrew and I worship the LORD, the God of heaven, who made the sea and the dry land." (Jonah 1:8–9)

> And should I not have concern for the great city of Nineveh, in which there are more than a hundred and twenty thousand people who cannot tell their right hand from their left—and also many animals? (Jonah 4:11).

Practical Applications for Your Life Today

- Is it wise to blame others for your choices and consequences?
- Do you ever let your bitterness keep you from honoring God?
- God has compassion not only for Jews but for all people, including you.
- Are you living your life in opposition to God?
- Never condemn or stand in judgment of a person who God loves.

- Do you only obey God's voice when it is convenient for you?
- Feel free to express both your positive and negative feelings toward God. He already knows what's in your heart and is willing to help you.
- Even when you are upset, God can still use you to accomplish something good for yourself and others.
- "God will bring every secret thing into judgment." This is why you need Jesus in your life—to cleanse you from all your sins.

Prayer

Dearest Heavenly Father, I would like you to provide me with the strength to change. I find myself seeking to gratify my fleshly desires instead of seeking what is best for my soul. Help me to come out of my state of denial and to realize that my actions affect everyone. Thank You for sparing my life and giving me the time and space to change. In Jesus' name, I pray. Amen!

MICAH

Judah: Before Captivity

Outline of the Book of Micah

1. Israel's and Judah's disruptive living brought God's judgment—Micah 1:1–2:13
2. Details injustices while sharing the deliverance of the helpless—Micah 3:1–5:15
3. Oppressors defeated while the promise of hope is given to others—Micah 6:1–7:20

In this book, God is taking His people to court as the lead prosecutor. The defendant is Israel, God is the judge, and heaven and earth are witnesses against Israel. The book of Micah is for everyone. If you are taking advantage of someone or you find yourself to be a victim, this book is for you. Many people unnecessarily raise prices, interest rates, and charge people more for repairs in today's society than they need to charge. God hits the gavel and issues his ruling on dishonesty. Read on and follow God, the transcripts of this court case, and see what happened to those who took advantage of people for personal gain.

The world is filled with corruption.

The officials took bribes.

The people tampered with the elections.

The government stopped aid to punish the innocent.

The government raised taxes.

The above headlines are the type of news that is being reported around the world. Long gone are the days when you could turn on your TV and watch exciting, compassionate, and informative news like someone helping their neighbor or a fireman helping a kitten out of a tree. Today everything is all about corruption, greed, money laundering, and a host of other depressing stories. If you are yearning for hope and truth, this is what Micah presents to you.

Micah was a prophet during a time when the people needed a message of hope and truth. God used him to warn the rulers to turn away from their corrupt and sinful ways. He urged the people to repent to avoid God's coming judgment. This warning primarily dealt with the northern kingdom (Israel). Micah also predicted the fall of the southern kingdom (Judah).

The wise man Solomon said, "There is nothing new under the sun" (Ecclesiastes 1:9). This statement is as true today as it was then. Today people behave in the same manner as those who lived many centuries ago during the time of Micah. People were spending their nights plotting how to take advantage of the less fortunate. They professed to be religious by helping people, but they were hypocrites. They used their religion as a vehicle for personal gain instead of for the goodness of God.

Because of hypocritical people, many make excuses for not seeking God. They will say, "I'm not religious, I'm spiritual," or "I don't go to church because they are a bunch of hypocrites." People with such a mindset have made either themselves, someone else, or something else their idol. However, on judgment day, everyone will have to give an account to God for his or her choices. God strongly opposes idol worshipers.

This self-centered behavior is identical to both Israel's and Judah's attitudes, which landed both kingdoms into captivity. God is fair. He has provided us guidelines to follow as He provided Israel and Judah. God wants to protect us from the negative consequences that come when we seek after our own will. Self-centeredness plus pride equals captivity. The northern kingdom would fall to Assyria, while the southern kingdom fell to Babylon.

Micah prophesied that Jesus would be born in Bethlehem. Through Jesus, a spiritual kingdom, the church was established. Jesus is the head of His church (Colossians 1:18). God wants everyone to be a part of His church. However, a person can only gain access to this kingdom by obeying the gospel of Jesus Christ.

My Verse for Golden Nuggets

> But you, Bethlehem Ephrathah, though you are small among the clans of Judah, out of you will come for me one who will be ruler over Israel, whose ori-

gins are from of old, from ancient times.
(Micah 5:2)

Listen to what the LORD says: "Stand
up, plead my case before the mountains;
let the hills hear what you have to say.
Hear, you mountains, the LORD's accu-
sation; listen, you everlasting foundations
of the earth. For the LORD has a case
against his people; he is lodging a charge
against Israel." (Micah 6:1–2)

He has shown you, O mortal, what is
good. And what does the Lord require of
you? To act justly and to love mercy and
to walk humbly with your God. (Micah
6:8)

Practical Applications for Your Life Today

- Have you ever cheated or taken advantage of
  someone for personal gain?
- Has anyone ever cheated or taken advantage of
  you? God knows.
- When God takes you to court, will Jesus be by
  your side defending you?
- Are you feeling oppressed? Take the high road,
  and turn your oppressors over to God.
- You may feel insignificant. However, God has
  greatness for you.

- False security will cause you to be taken captive by the enemy.
- Take a spiritual inventory; don't let others block you from God's blessings.

Prayer

Dear Heavenly Father, there is nothing new under the sun. What I am going through and everything that is happening is nothing new to You. Sometimes I feel insignificant. However, I know that You can use me for Your glory. My heart desires to do great things for You. Please help me. In Jesus' name, I pray. Amen.

NAHUM

To Nineveh, Capital City of Assyria: Before Judah's Captivity

Outline of the Book of Nahum

1. Nahum's message of anger against Nineveh—Nahum 1:1–15
2. The destruction of Nineveh is described—Nahum 2:1–13
3. The prophet gives reasons for judgment; woe to Nineveh—Nahum 3:1–19

Nahum's central message is one of comfort. God's people needed a significant dose of comfort for the severe and brutal violence inflicted on them by the Assyrians. This is why Nahum is bringing to you a message of comfort today. He is telling you that all will be well, even though attacks are relentlessly launched against you.

I think it is excellent that Nahum's name means "comfort." He was a prophet God used during this fearful time to comfort Judah. He prophesied against Assyria and its capital, Nineveh. Judah lived in constant fear of being overrun by their enemy.

If you remember Jonah's book, which took place about a hundred years earlier, God spared the Assyrians because they were willing to change their ways. However, this repentance and change of heart were short-lived, which is not what God wants. Shortly after Nahum's prophecy, Nineveh was plundered and crumbled by the Medes and Babylonians. God is powerful and fully able to help those who are oppressed and in trouble. Nothing goes unnoticed by God, and His timing is always perfect.

My Verses for Golden Nuggets

> The LORD is slow to anger but great in power; the LORD will not leave the guilty unpunished. His way is in the whirlwind and the storm, and clouds are the dust of his feet. (Nahum 1:3)

> The Lord is good, a refuge in times of trouble. He cares for those who trust in him. (Nahum 1:7)

Practical Applications for Your Life Today

- God has made you a guarantee that the guilty will not go unpunished.
- Are you thankful that God offers you a guilt-free way of living through His Son Jesus?
- You should always be mindful of the daily open communication between you and God.

- Repenting with an unchanging attitude or behavior is just reporting your sins.
- Do you want God to fight on your behalf?
- Learn how to identify the victories in your life and praise God for them.
- Never underestimate God; every one of His prophecies will be fulfilled.
- If you let your fears control you, how can you let faith grow you?
- When you trust in God and His promises, you will always have hope.

Prayer

Dearest Heavenly Father, You know everything that has happened to me and everything that ever will happen to me. I know that you are great and powerful. However, far too often, I allow fear and unforgiveness to paralyze my walk with You. I know that You can help me. In Jesus' name, I pray. Amen.

HABAKKUK

Judah: Before Captivity

Outline of the Book of Habakkuk

1. Habakkuk's first complaint and God's response—Habakkuk 1:1–11
2. Habakkuk's second complaint and God's response—Habakkuk 1:12–2:5
3. A song celebrating the fall of the Chaldeans—Habakkuk 2:6–20
4. Habakkuk's prayer—Habakkuk 3:1–19

Have you ever been tempted to question God? To ask, "Why God?" Well, don't worry, you are not alone. Habakkuk asked God questions when he didn't understand. The fantastic thing is that God answered his questions.

Habakkuk's prophecy is unique and unusual because he wrote about his conversation with God regarding the evil he saw all around him. He had some questions and doubts about God's judgment. The people of Judah were doing whatever they wanted without regard and respect for God. Habakkuk wanted to know why God didn't do something about Judah's disrespect.

To Habakkuk's surprise, God answered and explained that He would allow the Babylonians to invade Judah to punish them for their sins. This caused Habakkuk to ask more questions as to why God would use the wicked Babylonians to punish Judah. God assured Habakkuk that the Babylonians would also face punishment for their actions.

Judah was sent into brutal captivity as a consequence of not following God. Habakkuk then had a vision of God coming to save His people. Habakkuk resolved in his heart that no matter the circumstances, he would trust God. He believed that God would bring forth justice for His people.

Consequences and discipline are very much a part of God's nature. In the book of Hebrews, God is clear that He disciplines those He loves and accepts as children. If God does not discipline you, then you may be an illegitimate child. Yes, discipline seems unpleasant; however, it produces righteousness and peace (Hebrews 12:5–11).

My Verses for Golden Nuggets

> Then they sweep past like the wind and go on—guilty people, whose own strength is their god. (Habakkuk 1:11)

> Your eyes are too pure to look on evil; you cannot tolerate wrongdoing. Why then do you tolerate the treacherous? Why are you silent while the wicked

swallow up those more righteous than themselves? (Habakkuk 1:13)

Though the fig tree does not bud and there are no grapes on the vines, though the olive crop fails, and the fields produce no food, though there are no sheep in the pen and no cattle in the stalls, yet I will rejoice in the LORD, I will be joyful in God my Savior. The Sovereign LORD is my strength; he makes my feet like the feet of a deer, he enables me to tread on the heights. (Habakkuk 3:17–19)

Practical Applications for Your Life Today

- God can use any situation to get your attention.
- When you have questions and doubts, remember it's okay to talk with God.
- Make sure you have an open Bible and an open heart when conversing with God.
- Make sure your heart is attentive to your shortcomings, and work with God to overcome them.
- Do you realize that living for God brings about wonderful consequences?
- Remember God disciplines those whom He loves.

Prayer

Dearest Heavenly Father, Habakkuk has taught me that I can bring all my concerns to You. At times, I have allowed thoughts and behaviors to take me captive. As You delivered Your children long ago, I believe that You will also deliver me. In Jesus' name, I pray. Amen.

ZEPHANIAH

Judah: Before Captivity

Outline of the Book of Zephaniah

1. The prophet introduces himself and foretells judgment—Zephaniah 1:1–3
2. The day of the Lord will strike Judah and its neighbors—Zephaniah 1:4–18
3. God individually warns Judah and the nations—Zephaniah 2:1–3:8
4. The remnant will be restored—Zephaniah 3:9–20

Do you know that we are surrounded by idols every single day? By idols, I am not referring to graven images or sculptures. Here are some things that can quickly become idols: money, fame, relationships, cars, houses, careers, and even social media can become your idol. Anything you place in front of or before God is your idol. Your idol could also be your smartphone. No wonder they say that "we live in an era of smartphones and dull people."

The same way we worship many of these idols today, the people of Judah were involved in numerous forms of idol worship. Just like the prophet Joel, Zephaniah was always there to remind them of "the day of the Lord" when Jesus would return.

Zephaniah's words are still speaking to us today. He is reminding us that the day of the Lord is near. This book mentions the day of the Lord more than any other book in the Old Testament, including the major prophets. The day of the Lord had a dual fulfillment when Judah fell captive to the Babylonians, but it also refers to a future restoration and judgment from Jesus. In the same way, God brought severe judgment on the Israelites. God will also bring judgment on those who disobey Him today.

Zephaniah called for spiritual reform and warned the people that judgment would be brought against Judah and Jerusalem if the Jews refused to return to God. The prophet condemned idol worship and self-centered living. But upon hearing these warnings, the attitude of the people of Judah was one of complacency and denial. They foolishly felt that they were safe since God hadn't done anything yet. Zephaniah warned them that judgment would come not only to them but to the other nations around them if they refused to turn from their ungodly living. He was giving them a chance to change. It wasn't too late for them to change their ways. They needed to acknowledge, confess their sins, and get back on track with God. Praise God! The people listened to Zephaniah and experienced God's forgiveness to the fullest. Even though God said He would judge the proud and corrupt, He also promised to bless those who trusted Him until the end.

My verses for golden nuggets

> The great day of the Lord is near—
> near and coming quickly. Listen! The cry
> on the day of the Lord will be bitter,
> the Might Warrior shouts his battle cry.
> (Zephaniah 1:14)

> The LORD your God is with you, the
> Mighty Warrior who saves. He will take
> great delight in you; in his love he will no
> longer rebuke you, but will rejoice over
> you with singing. (Zephaniah 3:17)

> "At that time I will gather you; at that
> time I will bring you home. I will give you
> honor and praise among all the peoples
> of the earth when I restore your fortunes
> before your very eyes," says the LORD.
> (Zephaniah 3:20)

Practical Applications for Your Life Today

- Do you find it easy to place people, things, and situations before God?
- Do you ever struggle with being in denial?
- Are you feeling complacent in your walk with God?

- Are you one who says, "I believe in God," yet never take the time to pray, read, and implement what you have read?
- Would you like the Lord to rejoice over you with singing?
- Do you expect God to endorse your prideful and self-centered behaviors?
- It's useless to blame others for your poor choices.
- Live your life to be a godly influence in the lives of those around you.
- Be encouraged; the day of the Lord is closer than you think. Also, be ready.

Prayer

Dearest Heavenly Father, all around me are things that can become an idol to me. There are currently some things in my life that I need to eliminate. Please help me by giving me the necessary strength to confess those things that hinder my walk with You. In Jesus' name, I pray. Amen.

HAGGAI

After Judah's Captivity

Outline of the Book of Haggai

1. After God commands the rebuilding of the temple, the people take action—Haggai 1:1–15
2. God will fill the temple with His glory—Haggai 2:1–9
3. Disobedience brings disaster; obedience brings blessings—Haggai 2:10–19
4. Zerubbabel is told he will be chosen by God—Haggai 2:20–23

Has someone ever encouraged you to start something new after you failed an endeavor? Have you ever been inspired by someone to start a new relationship after a breakup? Has someone ever advised you to keep trying to lose weight despite several unsuccessful attempts? Well, that person is your Haggai.

Starting anew can be painful. It can be difficult to start learning how to walk again after having a leg amputation. It can be quite challenging to learn the ropes of managing a new business after your previous one collapsed; however, when you have a prophet like Haggai around, the work becomes a little easier because you have someone nearby to encourage you continually. Who is this Haggai?

Haggai was one of the prophets who encouraged the Jews to rebuild the temple after returning from their Babylonian captivity. King Cyrus decreed that the Jews could return home and begin rebuilding their temple. However, their work came to a halt when they met significant opposition from their neighbors. The Jewish people decided to stop building God's temple and devote their time to building their own houses. Not good!

Because they neglected to build God's house, the work that they were doing to restore their homeland ended up being useless. Because of their lack of action regarding rebuilding God's temple, they faced hardship in their personal lives. Haggai reminded them that they needed to dedicate themselves to completing the temple first. He let them know that failure to complete the temple was failing to honor God. He encouraged them to finish what God had requested of them. God promised that He would bless them if they continued working on the temple.

The Jewish people were inspired to complete rebuilding the temple, their community, and their lives. However, once the work was completed, the new temple was not as beautiful or glorious as the one Solomon built. Despite this, God told the people not to be discouraged. He promised that the new temple would be greater than the previous one because God would fill this temple with His glory.

My Verses for Golden Nuggets

"Is it a time for you yourselves to be living in your paneled houses, while this house remains a ruin?" Now this is what the LORD Almighty says: "Give careful thought to your ways." (Haggai 1:4–5)

Then Haggai, the Lord's messenger, gave this message of the Lord to the people: "'I am with you,' declares the Lord." (Haggai 1:13)

"Be strong, all you people of the land," declares the LORD, "and work. For I am with you,' declares the LORD Almighty." (Haggai 2:4)

Practical Applications for Your Life Today

- To whom is your allegiance, God or Satan? At this moment, it's one or the other. Remember, the devil owns the middle of the fence.
- Being committed and dedicated to God's work gets His attention.
- You will face unavoidable obstacles in rebuilding your life, but never fear. God knows your obstacles before you do, so why not allow Him to help you?

- Lack of forward progress will result in your life being taken over by the deceptions of this world.
- Building a life where you are spiritually healthy requires focusing on God's goodness instead of becoming distracted by negativity.
- You will never experience a fulfilled life apart from God.
- Get rid of any negative influences that are pulling you away from Jesus.
- Disobedience brings disaster; obedience brings laughter.
- Striving to put God first in your life is a wonderful way to live.

Prayer

Dearest Heavenly Father, I do not put You first as You deserve. Instead, I have allowed other negative influences to distract me. Please grant me the strength to take a stand and to build my life with You. You have promised that You will always be with me when I seek Your will for my life. In Jesus' name, I pray. Amen.

ZECHARIAH

After Judah's Captivity

Outline of the Book of Zechariah

1. Introduction—Zechariah 1:1–6
2. Zechariah's eight visions in the night—Zechariah 1:7–6:8
3. Zechariah crowns Joshua, son of Jozadak, the high priest—Zechariah 6:9–15
4. God's rules on fasting and promised blessings for Jerusalem—7:1–8:23
5. The Messiah is coming but will first be rejected—9:1–11:17
6. The Messiah will then come again, but this time, He will be accepted and will rule for all eternity—12:1–14:21

Some have been told that gaining college admission is not the most challenging aspect of acquiring education, and I agree. I have found the most challenging aspect of any endeavor is finishing what you start. How often have you started reading a book, only to lay it down and abandon it halfway through? How many times have you started a new diet plan only to quit before you accomplished your goal? Starting a new venture is not that difficult, for it takes minimal effort, but finishing strong can always be an issue. That is why God sent the prophet Zechariah to warn the people about the implications of abandoning the temple before they finished it.

Did they listen? You will have to find out.

Zechariah's name means "the Lord remembers." Zechariah's and Haggai's prophecies overlap each other. He encouraged those who were beginning to rebuild the temple to listen to God's message to them.

There was a lot of dysfunction in this community. Zechariah was there to lift their spirits and assure them that following God's instructions was the best course of action. This encouragement was very much needed as the builders wanted to give up. Their obedience to the Lord had a significant effect on their future. God promised that a Messiah would come and establish a final everlasting kingdom. Zechariah's message focused on getting people to see the importance of building the temple, their lives, and society.

My Verses for Golden Nuggets

> So he said to me, "This is the word of the LORD to Zerubbabel: 'Not by might nor by power, but by my Spirit,' says the LORD Almighty." (Zechariah 4:6)

"When I called, they did not listen; so when they called, I would not listen," says the LORD Almighty. (Zechariah 7:13)

Rejoice greatly, Daughter Zion! Shout, Daughter Jerusalem! See, your king comes to you, righteous and victorious, lowly and riding on a donkey, on a colt, the foal of a donkey. (Zechariah 9:9)

The Lord will be king over the whole earth. On that day there will be one Lord, and his name the only name. (Zechariah 14:9)

Practical Applications for Your Life Today

- It is not how you start the race that counts; what matters is how you finish.
- "You don't have to be great to get started; however, you must get started to become great."
- Strive every day to do the work of the Lord.
- An honest self-examination can lead to a positive spiritual transformation.
- Your future should hold no fear when God works on your behalf. He always keeps His promises.
- When you face disappointment, emptiness, and loneliness, remember God wants to fight your battles.

Prayer

Dearest Heavenly Father, thank You for reassuring me that You do remember and that You will never forget me. It's great to have encouragement from Your Word and fellow believers. I need to start rebuilding areas in my life with You. I understand that I will never be perfect. It is also wonderful to know that You do not expect perfection from me. However, that does not excuse my disobedience. Help me follow Your guidance for my life. In Jesus' name, I pray. Amen.

MALACHI

After Judah's Captivity

Outline of the Book of Malachi

1. God affirms His faithful love for Israel—Malachi 1:1–5
2. God rebukes Israel for their faithlessness toward Him—1:6–2:16
3. The Lord announces He is coming both to judge and reward—2:17–4:6

Have you ever been robbed or had something stolen from you? If you have, then you know the feeling of being violated. With that in mind, Malachi posed this question to God's people, "Will a man rob God?" Let's see why Malachi asked this question.

Malachi wrote this final Old Testament book about eighty years after the temple had been rebuilt. People became impatient because Jesus, the promised Messiah, had not come. They had a casual attitude toward God and began offering Him unacceptable sacrifices. Instead of giving God their best, they offered animals that were diseased, crippled, and blind for a sacrifice.

"Is that not wrong?" God asked them. He told them to try giving these sick animals to their governor to see if he would be pleased. Yet they continuously showed disrespect to God by offering these kinds of sacrifices to Him. They reaped the consequences of their disrespect in the form of poor crops, economic depression, and attacks by raiders. The leaders failed to hold themselves and God's people accountable.

The second part of Malachi's message was one of forgiveness and hope. Malachi informed the Israelites of God's promise to send a prophet who would turn the people's hearts back to God if they were repentant. This promise was fulfilled by the coming of John the Baptist, who prepared the way for Jesus, the long-awaited Messiah. Malachi emphasized the importance of turning away from sin and renewing their covenant with God. To the faithful, God promised that they would be spared from the coming judgment, but He vowed to destroy the unfaithful.

My Verses for Golden Nuggets

> "When you offer blind animals for sacrifice, is that not wrong? When you sacrifice lame or diseased animals, is that not wrong? Try offering them to your governor! Would he be pleased with you? Would he accept you?" says the LORD Almighty. (Malachi 1:8)

> I will send my messenger, who will prepare the way before me. (Malachi 3:1)

"Will a man rob God? Yet you rob me. But you ask, 'How are we robbing you?'" "In tithes and offerings." (Malachi 3:8)

Practical Applications for Your Life Today

- Have you ever considered how you are robbing God today?
- Living a daily life of instant gratification will definitely leave you spiritually bankrupt.
- Try to honor God with all your possessions.
- If there is faulty leadership, continue following God; don't make excuses.
- Pursuing ungodly and unhealthy relationships will cause you to stray away from God.
- The promise of Jesus' return should provide you hope.

Prayer

Dear Heavenly Father, thank You for Your love and the compelling examples You have left me. I can look at my life and see how I have robbed You by not giving You my best. I've been guilty of seeking instant gratification instead of seeking spiritual edification from You. Please forgive me and help me bring glory to You in all that I do.

In Jesus' name, I pray. Amen.

*****

Following Malachi, there begins what is known as the four hundred years of silence. This refers to the period between the Old Testament and the New Testament. During this period, God ceased speaking to the Jewish people through prophets.

However, during these four hundred years, there were changes in the different world powers. Remember, before the Old Testament ended, the Persian Empire conquered both the Assyrians and Babylonians. Then the Greek Empire conquered the Persian Empire. Then the Roman Empire, in turn, conquered the Greek Empire and became the new dominant world power.

Even though God's voice was silent for four hundred years, His hand was clearly directing the course of history. At just the right time, Jesus, the long-awaited Messiah, was born as prophesied into a Jewish family through the tribe of Judah. His message of salvation to the world was written precisely in the Greek language, which was the universal language at that time. How wonderful it is that God has preserved copies of the New Testament scriptures in its original Greek language today. Thank You, Jesus!

*****

Wow! Look, you have made it through the last book of the Old Testament. Hopefully, you have learned a lot along the way, or perhaps you used this book as a refresher. I pray that this is not the end of your quest to study the wonderful Word of God. Instead, I hope it is a new beginning and that you can now clearly see God's love for you.

Please recommend or gift a copy of this book to help someone else better understand the Old Testament. When you gain knowledge, it is like water coming into a lake. If it stops flowing, it becomes stagnant. So share what you have learned and watch how you and others will grow in God.

Remember, "It is more blessed to give than it is to receive" (Acts 20:35).

ARE YOU MISSING OUT ON YOUR INHERITANCE?

What Inheritance?

When you become a Christian, you become God's child. Through the church, you are adopted into His family, which is the everlasting kingdom that Jesus purchased with His own blood. God's promise to you is that when you become His child, you become an heir of God, not only that, you become coheirs or joint-heirs with Christ.

Amazing and true!

Here is an earthly example. In our society, we have what is known as a will. A person goes to an attorney and makes a will outlining how to distribute their earthly possessions to their heirs. When that person dies, his or her wishes are implemented. This means that the people listed in the will are known as inheritors. They are legally entitled to the things promised in the will.

This is no different from how the Bible explains a will. "Because a will is in force only when somebody has died; it never takes effect while the one who made it is living" (Hebrews 9:17). This is why Jesus died so that you and I could be sons and daughters of God's inheritance. "An inheritance that can never perish, spoil or fade. This inheritance is kept in heaven for you." Thank You, Jesus!

Please read Acts 20:28, Galatians 4:4–7, Romans 14:12–17, and 1 Peter 1:3–4.

God's Plan of Salvation, Not Man's

God has been clear on His plan for humanity from the very beginning. Today is no different. His plan to save you and me is clear. Just read the following scriptures.

The Scriptures are very clear about what it takes to become a child of God. Here is the simple plan revealed in God's word:

Step 1: We must *hear* the Word. Without first hearing God's Word, we would never know that we are sinners and that the "wages of sin" is death (Romans 3:23, Romans 6:23). Without hearing, we wouldn't know of Jesus' sacrifice for our sins and our need for Him. It's also where our faith comes from (Romans 10:17). Further, we should only listen to Jesus as our Savior (Matthew 17:5, Hebrews 1:1–2, Matthew 28:18).

Step 2: We must *believe* what we have heard. Merely hearing the Word of God doesn't save anyone. We must believe what we hear, or we are not likely to obey God's commands. In John 8:24, Jesus says, "If you believe not that I am He, you will die in your sins." Belief is not enough. James 2:24 says we must "do" what God asks. This is His will for our lives (Matthew 7:21).

Step 3: We must *repent* of our sins. Sin is what separates us from God (Isaiah 59:2). Therefore, if we intend to seek God's forgiveness, we must be willing to strive to turn away from our old behaviors. Repentance means "turning away from sin" and making an effort to sin no more (1 Corinthians 6:9–11). If we aren't willing to repent of our sins, we cannot be saved (Acts 3:19, Acts 17:30–31).

Step 4: We must *confess* our faith. Those that wish to be saved must confess their faith in Jesus (Romans 10:9–10). It was Jesus Christ Himself who said, "Whosoever therefore shall confess me before men, him will I confess also before my Father which is in heaven" (Matthew 10:32). The Scriptures give us an example of one who confessed their faith (Acts 8:26–39, note verse 37).

Step 5: We must be *baptized*. There is considerable religious confusion about baptism. Some think baptism isn't necessary. Others believe we are saved before we are baptized. Note what the Scriptures say baptism does:

- Baptism shows a good conscience toward God. The Apostle Peter clearly confirms, "baptism does also now save us" (1 Peter 3:21).
- Baptism washes away sins (Acts 22:16).
- Baptism gives entry "into" Christ (Romans 6:3, Galatians 3:27).
- Jesus, our authority, made baptism necessary when He gave the command in Mark 16:16. In other words, our sins are not washed away, and we are not "in Christ" until we are baptized.

- Since baptism is for the forgiveness of sins (Acts 2:38), we are still in our sins (and lost) until we are baptized.
- We should also realize that baptism is a burial or immersion, not sprinkling (Romans 6:3–4), and baptism is for believers, not infants (Mark 16:16).
- Many people say, "We aren't saved by works!" Is baptism a work? It is a work of God (Colossians 2:12). Jesus says belief is a work too (John 6:29). James says we must have faith plus works (James 2:14–26, note verse 24). God's mercy and grace save us, but He demands we be baptized to wash away our sins. He does the work through His Son's blood if we follow His instructions.

Step 6: We must remain *faithful*. While baptism puts us into Christ and His blood washes away our sins, we must still be obedient and faithful to God. Otherwise, we will lose our souls. The Bible tells us, "Be faithful unto death, and I will give you the crown of life" (Revelation 2:10).

If you haven't met these conditions and want to obey the gospel of Jesus, please contact me at Godsvirtualschool@ gmail.com or polishingthepeople@gmail.com.

GLOSSARY

ark of the covenant. A beautifully crafted chest that contained the golden pot that had manna, Aaron's rod that budded, and the tablets of the covenant.

concubines. Like a secondary wife. They bore children for the husband, especially when the wife could not conceive.

covenant. A mutual agreement between God and His people. God gives His guidance, His protective care, His assurance, and His presence. However, to partake in these blessings requires obedience and loyalty to God alone.

Hebrew. An individual who is a descendant of Abraham; it means the same as an Israelite or Jew.

Isaac. The son of Abraham and the father of Jacob.

Israel. The name God gave to Jacob following his wrestling with the angel. Jacob had twelve sons and their descendants became the twelve tribes of Israel or the Israelites. They are also sometimes referred to as the nation of Israel. Israel is both a name and a geographical location.

Israelites. A Jew, a Hebrew, and descendant of Abraham.

Judah. Jacob's fourth son. His descendants were known as the tribe of Judah. It was also the name of the land

HARRY C. WASHINGTON III

in which they lived following the division of the kingdoms. Judah was located in the southern kingdom.

Levites. The tribe chosen by God to be the priesthood. They were descendants of Levi, one of the twelve sons of Jacob.

manna. An edible substance God provided to the Israelites for food during their forty years in the wilderness. It tasted like wafers made with honey. The Bible describes it as "angel's food" in Psalm 78:25.

patriarch. The name given to the founding fathers of the Hebrew/Jewish race.

pharaoh. Title of Egyptian ruler or king.

promised land. Canaan, the land promised by God to Abraham and his descendants. An area that included parts of modern-day Israel, Palestine, Lebanon, Syria, and Jordan.

prophet. One who speaks for God.

prophecy. A declaration that speaks God's truth in the present about things that are often revealed in the future.

tabernacle. A temporary tent structure. It was a portable place for worship before the temple was built.

wilderness. Generally, a rocky and barren desert. Moses and the Israelites wandered in the wilderness. Moses died within sight of the Promised Land on Mount Nebo.

*****

It is also worth knowing that the vast majority of the Old Testament took place in the region we know today as the Middle East. This region covers three continents. Although primarily in western Asia, the Middle East also encompasses parts of northern Africa and southeastern Europe. Here are some present-day countries in this region: Iraq, Iran, Saudi Arabia, Jordan, Israel, Syria, and Turkey.

The Bible is like a complete road map for mankind's relationship with God. From the beginning, God entered into a covenant relationship with man. He made promises and prophecies that have been fulfilled. All prophecies will be completed when Jesus comes for the final judgment day.

ABOUT THE AUTHOR

Harry C. Washington III resides in Tennessee with his adorable wife, Audrey. Harry has two children, nine grandchildren, and two great-grandchildren. He retired from the United States Air Force after serving twenty years defending the faith and freedom of the United States of America. All to the glory of God! Before retiring from full-time ministry, Harry ministered at the Outreach Church of Christ for twenty years. He was also the founder and director of Christian Grace Counseling Center and Christian Grace Counseling Academy during this time. He provided biblically based counseling that focuses on heart issues and not simply the symptoms. The Christian Counseling Academy provides training opportunities for others to become licensed Christian counselors.

He received his doctorate in philosophy and clinical Christian counseling from Cornerstone University. He received his master's degree in Bible and ministry from Lubbock Christian University. He also obtained a bachelor's degree in psychology with a minor in sociology as well as a bachelor's degree in criminal justice from Columbia College. In addition, he received his associate degree in business administration from Southwestern Christian College and two other associate degrees from the Community College of the Air Force.

Harry, at a very young age, wanted to make the world a better place. He has dedicated his life to using his God-given talents to provide hope, help, and healing to the hurting. Harry strives to be an open book about his struggles with sin. He will never forget how talking to someone about the deepest and darkest of his struggles with sin brought about true healing and hope in his life. Harry believes with all his heart to "confess your sins to each other and pray for each other so that you may be healed" (James 5:16). Harry teaches that living for Jesus is the absolute best way to live life. He knows that all sins were nailed to the cross. He encourages others to live in the forgiveness and freedom of Jesus. He enjoys building stronger Christian families and has worked extensively with children for nearly fifty years. Harry and Audrey enjoy traveling the world together, exploring different cultures, sharing Christ's love, and meeting fellow believers. He is now a Christian motivational speaker and a Christian YouTuber. His channels are *God's Virtual School, God's Greater Love, Polishing The People,* and *Christ's Kids 4Ever.* You can reach Harry at Godsgreaterlove@gmail.com.

CPSIA information can be obtained
at www.ICGtesting.com
Printed in the USA
BVHW050228170423
662378BV00006B/165